Ferdinand Marcos and the Philippines

The Political Economy of Authoritarianism

ALBERT F. CELOZA

Westport, Connecticut
London

Library of Congress Cataloging-in-Publication Data

Celoza, Albert F.
    Ferdinand Marcos and the Philippines : the political economy of
authoritarianism / Albert F. Celoza.
       p. cm.
    Includes bibliographical references and index.
    ISBN 0–275–94137–X (alk. paper)
    1. Authoritarianism—Philippines. 2. Bureaucracy—Philippines.
3. Patronage, Political—Philippines. 4. Philippines—Politics and
government—1946–1973. 5. Philippines—Politics and
government—1973–1986. 6. Marcos, Ferdinand E. (Ferdinand Edralin),
1917– . I. Title.
JQ1416.C45   1997
320.9599′09′047—dc21   96–37732

British Library Cataloguing in Publication Data is available.

Library of Congress Catalog Card Number: 96–37732
ISBN: 0–275–94137–X

First published in 1997

Praeger Publishers, 88 Post Road West, Westport, CT 06881
An imprint of Greenwood Publishing Group, Inc.

Printed in the United States of America

The paper used in this book complies with the
Permanent Paper Standard issued by the National
Information Standards Organization (Z39.48–1984).

10 9 8 7 6 5 4 3 2 1

Contents

Acknowledgments

Gratitude is owed to many for the completion of this work. Praeger Publishers expressed interest in and ultimately published this book; Ann Celoza, Cynthia Engvall, Richard Gaffin, Jim Gould, Zeddick Lanham, Norine Mudrick, and Patricia Nay extended editorial, research, technical and production assistance. Bob Sullivan, Social Science Department Chair at Phoenix College, provided a hospitable environment for my academic pursuits; the faculty and staff of the Program for Southeast Asian Studies at Arizona State University granted funding and support for this particular work; and, Ann, my wife and friend, without whom all that I have accomplished would not have been possible.

Chapter 1

Introduction

On February 26, 1986, Ferdinand Marcos, the man who ruled the Philippines for almost twenty years, left the presidential palace amidst a throng of people rallying for his removal. A military group, led by longtime Marcos ally Juan Ponce-Enrile, had declared a rebellion, which the people enthusiastically supported. A quick overthrow of Marcos had been unexpected. After the assassination of Marcos's chief rival, Benigno Aquino, in August 1983, many predicted that the Marcos government would not survive the crisis resulting from that assassination. In spite of the predictions of his political demise, however, Marcos did survive massive opposition for a few more years.

During the early 1980s a general feeling prevailed that no alternative to Marcos and his regime existed and that his hold on power was strong in spite of the widespread criticism against him. In 1981 he was able to lift martial law and still retain his absolute powers. Martial law was no longer necessary to justify his rule because he had established his power base.

This study explains how the authoritarian regime of Marcos ruled the Philippines and remained in power after the coup of 1972. This study also will look into the means that Marcos employed to maintain his power. Repressive regimes may seem undesirable, but they are able to elicit the support of significant sectors of society. Marcos was able to maintain authoritarian rule because of the support of bureaucrats, businesspeople, the military, and political leaders in various regions, with the assistance of the U.S. government. He maintained this network of support through a patron-client system with a centralized bureaucracy as its power and resource base. In order to reward his supporters, Marcos expanded the authority of government. To minimize the political cost of the expansion, he maintained the legal and constitutional forms of democracy. To add credibility to his usurpation of power, he claimed that economic development was impossible without centralized authority. Government information offices and the controlled media echoed his claims and extolled the virtues of the regime. To discourage, weaken, and punish his opponents, Marcos used the armed forces and paramilitary groups who arrested and imprisoned more than 60,000 citizens and harassed or liquidated alleged subversives. To assure survival and the enjoyment of patronage, various sectors of society capitulated to the Marcos government. Marcos's network of supporters wanted benefits, favors, and protection; in turn, Marcos needed their support, so the interests of Marcos and his supporters converged in order to make an authoritarian regime possible.

The Philippine experience in authoritarian rule is not unique. Most Third World countries are being ruled by authoritarian governments; in fact, most countries of the world do not have democratic political systems. Democracy in these instances is understood as "a political system which supplies regular constitutional opportunities for changing government officials, and a social mechanism which permits the largest possible part of the population to influence major decisions by choosing among contenders for political office."[1] Some leaders of authoritarian governments attained their positions of leadership through election; however, many were installed after prevailing in a power struggle among the strongest competing groups.

How do authoritarians maintain themselves in power? A commonsense answer may be that their ruthlessness and repression silences or eliminates opposition. One cannot deny that a government's violence against its own citizens works toward maintaining a government's power. Humans hesitate to act when they know that their acts may result in torture or death. Marcos certainly employed terrorist tactics against his opponents, but can terror alone explain the staying power of regimes? Many regimes, despite repressive tactics, were unable to maintain themselves. When thinking of the control systems set up by authoritarians, one has to take into account that these systems entail costs. If, for some reason, a dictator cannot find the money to pay the costs of his repression, his regime will not be able to resist opposition.

Another possible explanation for authoritarian power holds that economic development in underdeveloped countries is possible only under the close direction of a centralized authority. Proponents claim that if the society is to progress economically, order must be established and certain practices (usually of a feudal nature) must be reformed to make progress possible. Such "progress" in a society is painful, and a centralized authority needs to curb liberty in order to ensure that order is established and maintained in spite of the pain. Marcos eloquently justified his establishment of order:

The primary problem in many modernizing societies is not liberty but the creation of a legitimate public order. Men may, of course, have order without liberty, but they cannot have liberty without order. Authority has to exist before it can be limited, and it is authority that is in scarce supply in those modernizing countries where government is at the mercy of alienated intellectuals, rambunctious colonels, and rioting students.[2]

An authoritarian regime, it is claimed, may enjoy the support of the people if the people believe they are making progress. There may be some truth to the claim, but the people's belief in the benefits of authoritarian rule is insufficient to maintain an authoritarian in power.

Closely tied to the idea that order precedes liberty is the idea that nationalism requires authoritarian rule. It has only been since World War II that most Third World countries have gained independence from colonial powers. In many cases, the colonial period damaged the national psyche, and a sense of national pride was lost. Authoritarians claim that to make the nation great again, citizens must rally around a leader who will lead them to a proud and prosperous future. Authoritarians further claim that prosperity can be had only if unity of purpose is created and maintained in the nation. Internal squabbling, such as in Marcos's regime, is seen as incompatible with nationalism. Nationalism implies a certain degree of homogeneity.

To complicate things further, when the colonialists withdrew, they often left behind national boundaries that ignored the ethnic, linguistic, and religious characters of the inhabitants; so groups of peoples, with little in common except their subjugation by colonialists, would then have to make common cause. Usually, they only "made" divisiveness, so the authoritarian would establish himself as the only one who could arbitrate disputes and give the country unity. Such unity, incidentally, usually came at the expense of ethnic groups with no ties to the leader. The myth of nationalism, therefore, may foster support for a dictator, but it does not explain his staying power.

When one looks at the tactics of the Marcos regime, one sees that terror, repression, and nationalistic rhetoric about the need for order did not constitute a major source of power. Rather, they were part of a large number of tactics Marcos used to make the economic, social, and political costs of resisting his regime greater than those of not resisting. Other tactics included democratic formalities, bribes, patronage, control of the media, and consolidation of bureaucratic power. Marcos employed a mix of those tactics that, with the least possible cost to himself, enabled him to satisfy the needs of key power elites within Philippine society. The mutual support between Marcos and various power elites is the key to understanding his grip on power. As long as supporting Marcos was profitable to the elites, he stayed in power. When at the end of his rule the costs exceeded the profits, Marcos was removed.

POLITICS AS ECONOMIC BEHAVIOR

Political power and its benefits (public or private) are commodities like any other. They are therefore subject to the laws of supply and demand, and of marginal utility. Further, the individual exists before the group; thus group formation and group action can be understood only as a function of the individual pursuit of self-interest by group members. Such economic explanations have proven to be powerful tools for understanding various aspects of the political process in Western democracies, shedding light on the formation of interest groups, the conduct of bureaucracies, the behavior of politicians and voters, and the role of government.

Although the Philippines is not a Western democracy, the economic insights applied to politics in the West can, with some modification, be applied to understanding the interactions of the power elites in the Philippines. Philippine politics had been largely non-ideological, consisting mainly of power groups jockeying with one another for the fruits of political patronage. Parties were just a means of facilitating bids for power. Politicians bought support with promises of benefits. Marcos made promises, but he circumvented the electoral and legal systems, appealing directly to those groups with sufficient economic and feudal power to sustain his position. As long as the needs of those groups were met, Marcos maintained his power.

Before proceeding to apply economic analysis to the Philippines, a few relevant points are necessary in order to understand how groups form in society. First, groups who successfully work together for a common good (including interest groups) are groups where the costs of membership to the individual are less than either the benefits of membership or the costs of nonmembership. Individuals will not be involved in creating a public, common good if their individual costs exceed the individual benefit from that good, nor will they willingly share in the burden of producing a common good if they can attain the good for free by letting others produce it. The ironic result is that many groups with common interests will not act together. If the costs of mobilizing a group to action to produce a common good are greater to the ones who mobilize the group than the benefits that will result, the individuals will not mobilize the group, and the group will not form. No one will then act, and all will be worse off.[3] Group formation and action are also affected by access to information. Before a group can act, it must understand the forces that affect its goals. In the case of political interest groups, the government is the primary "force" that needs to be understood. Before a group will act, it must be apparent to that group what the effect of a government policy will be and how it will affect the group. Information is never perfect, and government seems always to want to obscure the effects of policy when it will adversely affect a given group. One of the costs involved in group activity, then, is obtaining information and overcoming the attempts at disinformation by the government or by other groups. Those groups that do obtain information for themselves then try to conceal information from potential rivals. Groups who do not act together are unable or unwilling to bear the cost of getting information.

A second key element in applying an economic analysis to the Philippines is that politicians and constituents can be viewed as sellers and buyers in a market. The politicians are selling goods and services from public resources. In exchange, they look for votes or other forms of support from constituents. The link between constituent support on the one hand and governmental services on the other is indirect. The constituents, in effect, "buy" the supplier (politician) rather than the goods themselves. Politicians, in turn, have to provide a selection of goods and services without the benefit of direct feedback, which will satisfy their constituents and thus enable the politicians to remain in power. The lack of direct feedback leads politicians to provide services that offer the greatest likelihood of winning support.

One way to win this support is by providing services characterized by a clear benefit to a small group while, at the same time, characterized by unclear costs to society as a whole. The small group will try to support the politician who provides it services because the benefit of those services is clear. The general public pays but may not even be aware that it is paying. However, the cost is likely to be small enough that even if constituents knew they were paying, they would not try to change the situation anyway. The result is that the politician has a small but dedicated group on his side, with no one opposed. The group also will likely make donations to the politician so that he in turn can use media and other services to seek further support.

Votes have usually been seen as the medium of exchange in the political marketplace in Western-style democracies. Although the Philippines has democratic structures and procedures—including elections—ethnic and feudal relationships play the dominant role in determining political power. To govern effectively, the ruler of the Philippines needs the support of key families. Those families are landowners who have extensive control over those areas of the country where their plantations and businesses are located. Local government officials usually owe their positions to the influence of the local family, so they are reluctant to oppose them. The leader of the Philippines, then, must be able to adopt policies that favor the ruling elites. Marcos sustained himself through elections for thirteen years because he satisfied the demands of key power groups. In keeping with the second principle mentioned above, Marcos satisfied the demands of a relatively small group of people using the resources of the Philippines as a whole so the small groups benefited while most citizens saw their wages lessen and the infrastructure of the nation slowly deteriorate. In keeping with the first principle mentioned above, most citizens, even though they may have been aware of the gradual decline in his living standard, were unable to offer any resistance because they were unable to sustain the cost necessary to depose Marcos. They could not sustain the cost because they lacked the economic resources to publicize their cause in spite of media distortion. Marcos finally used repressive force to make protesters pay the ultimate price. The costs of resistance outweighed the benefits. The average citizen also was unwilling to bear the cost of resistance because the political power of the elites ensured that those outside the elites had no real chance to gain power. Resistance could then have likely resulted only in one elite dictator replacing another.

A group can be expected to resist a dictator only when it has the chance to usurp his position. The communists were an exception, being members of a nonelite group willing to put up resistance. The nature of the communist revolution and ideology is such that the rebels saw themselves as replacing the dictator. They fought not to change the system but to establish a new system. For the communists, then, the ultimate gain was perceived to be greater than the immediate costs.

In the Philippines, it was finally an elite group who overthrew Marcos. Corazon Aquino was supported by members of powerful families who believed that the Philippine economy in the 1980s was destroying their wealth. They could no longer support Marcos and sought to usurp his power so that they could retain their profitable positions.

Various theories and models may be used to understand human behavior. I have chosen those of history and economics in order to understand the politics of the Philippines. Although we try to be objective or descriptive about our subject, the line between prescription and description is fuzzy. This is not so much that we are unable to distinguish between what is and what ought to be. It is that our descriptive theories hold prescriptive consequences. According to its simplifications, human behavior is described as self-interested and wealth-maximizing. I am afraid that one prescriptive result of this point of view is that to behave out of other than crass self-interest is "irrational" and opens one up to exploitation by others. I do not believe that the pursuit of the ideals of justice or equality is pointless unless undergirded by economic self-interest. Economics and political science describe how we do, in fact, behave. We are not constrained to behave this way.

NOTES

1. Seymour Martin Lipset, *Political Man: The Social Bases of Politics* (New York: Anchor Books, Doubleday and Co., 1963), p. 28.

2. Ferdinand E. Marcos, *The Democratic Revolution in the Philippines*, 2nd ed. (Englewood Cliffs, NJ: Prentice Hall International, 1979), pp. 263-264.

3. Mancur Olson, *The Logic of Collective Action: Public Goods and the Theory of Groups* (Cambridge, MA: Harvard University Press, 1971).

Chapter 2

A Nation Divided

Divide et impera: Divide and conquer. The Philippines stands as "a nation divided against itself: divided between urban and rural, rich and poor, majorities and minorities, privileged and underprivileged."

—Ferdinand E. Marcos

Divided by natural barriers, mountains and bodies of water, diverse languages and dialects, and ethnic cultures, the group of islands located on the Pacific rim of Asia were easily conquered by the colonial powers. The strategic location of the Philippines, as well as the area's rich natural resources, has attracted world powers since the sixteenth century. General Arthur MacArthur, father of Douglas MacArthur and military governor-general of the Philippines, described the unique strategic potential of the Philippines as "the finest group of islands in the world," whose "strategic location is unexcelled by that of any position in the globe."[1]

The Philippine archipelago is composed of some 7,100 islands spread over approximately 496,400 square nautical miles. It has a total land area of 300,000 square kilometers with one of the world's longest coastlines.[2] Most settlements are found in coastal areas, the rest in the mountains, creating a dichotomy between lowlanders and uplanders (*taga-bundok*). Sociocultural changes took place more rapidly in coastal areas than in the mountains. Those changes set the lowland Filipinos apart from their mountain-dweller kin and produced another dichotomy: the majority and the minority.[3] The majority was more exposed to Western and Christian influences, whereas the minority "maintained the greatest links with their indigenous cultural heritage and . . . least accepted the colonial structures imposed by the Spanish."[4] Other factors contributed to the differences between the city and the countryside. The countryside (*probinsya*) depended on farming and fishing, whereas the cities controlled the industries and business. Manila, the principal city and capital of the Philippines, is the political, economic, and cultural center of the country. Each year hordes of migrants from the provinces flock to the city. The city's glittering lights, its apparent promise of opportunity, and the harsh conditions of the provinces encouraged migration.

Enclaves for the rich and the poor are strewn throughout the crowded and polluted city. In one study an estimated 1.8 million people, or 30% of Manila's residents, live in slums.[5] According to a study by the West German government,

34% to 40% of the population of Manila are squatters.[6] Poverty pervades the areas where houses are usually made of cardboard and scrap materials. Some dwellings are even constructed over stagnant water. According to a World Bank report, "The 1977 urban poverty income estimated for the Philippines was P1,877 ($250) per person per year. Thirty-nine percent of families in slums of major cities have per capita income below that sum. In metropolitan Manila, 35 percent of the population, or about 2.1 million people, live below the poverty level; they account for 30 percent of the urban poor in the Philippines."[7] No one can escape the contrast between the hovels by railroad tracks and muddy canals and the big houses secured by high walls and guarded by dogs and armed security guards.

Another important dichotomy among Filipinos is the shade of their skins: mestizo or non-mestizo. Mestizos are individuals of mixed parentage—Filipino mixed with either Chinese, Spanish, or American. Usually of fairer complexion, mestizos are prevalent among the wealthier classes.

There are at least eight (lowland) ethnolinguistic groups and an array of other dialect subgroups. Manila is the capital and the center of the Tagalog region, so speakers are perceived as culturally superior by others as well as by themselves. The speakers of Cebuanos are the most numerous native speakers, but most Filipinos are at least familiar with Tagalog, the language of the capital city.

Within ethnolinguistic groups, one finds variations that cause subtle if not obvious ethnocentric biases; for example, Tagalog is spoken by most inhabitants of central and southern Luzon, but one finds differences in accent, vocabulary, and some traditions in each town or municipality. One can see these differences even in towns separated by only a few miles. Stereotypes within and among ethnic groups develop. Members of the same ethnic groups tend to cluster in Manila's universities, in some urban settlements, and in neighborhoods and civic organizations.

Despite their ethnic diversity, most Filipinos conform to a single religion. The Philippines is a predominantly Roman Catholic country; most Filipinos are baptized Catholics. Some 85% profess Catholicism, 5% are Muslims, and the remaining 10% are composed of various religions, including other Christian denominations such as the Philippine Independent Church, *Iglesia ni Kristo* (Church of Christ), the Methodist church, and other Protestant groups.[8] Though Christianity and Islam have been in the Philippines for more than 300 years, folk religions or animistic beliefs such as spiritism are still practiced. Filipinos "filipinized" Christianity and Islam and blended them with their indigenous rituals and practices.[9] In towns where were founded "new" churches, such as the Philippine Independent Church, conflicts arose. Religious differences among inhabitants carried over into other facets of life, such as civic projects, fiestas, and other celebrations, and politics.

Comprising only 5% of the population, Muslim Filipinos are insignificant in number, but they exert a considerable force in Philippine society.[10] Spanish colonizers were unable to subjugate them completely. The Muslims waged such fierce battles against the Americans that the garrand automatic rifle had to be invented to put down *juramentados* (those running amok). The relationship of the Muslims with the central government in Manila has not been uniformly cordial either. Concentrated mostly in Southern Mindanao and Sulu, Muslims live far from the center of government, so they feel remote from the mainstream of Filipino politics. Their separation, resulting from history, geography, and culture, has created tensions between them and other Filipinos. During the 1950s, many Filipinos from Luzon and Visayas settled in Mindanao, then considered "the Philippine frontier." Because of its vast, rich, and unexploited natural resources, the region was called the "land of promise." The influx of migrants resulted in conflicts. Immigrants and natives clashed as they competed for the control of land. In the 1970s, foreign corporations in Mindanao exacerbated the situation.[11]

Religious differences were only one of the factors contributing to the conflicts in Mindanao. In communal strife, it is easy to point to religious differences, but the situation was more complex. Terrorist groups and private armed bands, soldiers and the various Muslim factions, all were in conflict. The Muslims themselves were divided into some ten major subgroups, the principal group being the Maguindanaos, the Maranaos, and the Tausogs. Traditionally, they had been separately governed under two sultanates: those of Maguindanao and Sulu.[12]

Economic and social classes, however, were not as numerous or as complex as ethnic diversities. Most people lived below the poverty line. Only a few families controlled the wealth of the region. The gap between rich and poor has not narrowed over the years but has widened in spite of the relative increase in gross national product during the 1970s; social mobility has come to a standstill.

The many variations, differences, and disparities are unified by a political entity called the Philippines. One can appropriately refer to the Philippines in the singular and in the plural "because . . . the name refers both to an island archipelago and to a unified nation with a single people and a highly fragmented and plural[istic] society."[13] As a national entity it declared its political independence on June 12, 1898.[14] While its independence from Spain was being proclaimed, the first republic in Asia was already threatened by the occupying forces of the United States. In its infancy, the emergent nation was stifled internally by its inherent differences. Still emerging as a nation, the Philippines remains rife with ethnic and class loyalties that often take precedence over national interest or allegiance.

Fred Eggan, a noted anthropologist, observed that the basic problem of the Philippines has been to develop and maintain enough unity to overcome the forces making for division. For many periods in Philippine history the question of whether the Philippines would exist as a unit or be broken up into regions, or into religious groups, has been a serious one.[15]

Since the latter nineteenth century, nationalism has been important to Philippine history, but even up to the present time, it remains a weak force compared to the hold of ethnicity and patron-client relationships. Ideologies little influence political behavior. In the pursuit of power and influence, the network of alliances founded through patrons and clients plays the more dominant role. Interest in tangible rewards far surpasses ideas in attracting and bringing peoples together. In a "nation divided against itself,"[16] rulers do not have to create dissensions. In a nation where nationalism and ideology are still developing, authority and obedience can be established by giving or withholding tangible rewards and by threatening to use force and punishment; thus, Philippine history and society have been molded by allegiances to the nation and to the group. More often than not the latter prevails, and at certain times the consequences of the prevalence have not been beneficial to national interests.

LAS ISLAS FILIPINAS: A SPANISH COLONIAL OUTPOST

Pre-Hispanic Philippine society was composed of independent communities called *barangays*. There was no central ruler or government, although some settlements did form alliances and groupings. Each village was headed by a *datu* or headman. Sufficient food was produced for consumption. Land was communal, although each farmer tilled a parcel for himself. Trade by barter was conducted among villages as well as with people from far-away places such as China. Although early chronicles allude to slavery, early servitude was more in the nature of service in exchange for gratitude and protection than indentured slavery.[17] Pre-Hispanic Philippine religion was animistic, but by the fifteenth century, Filipinos in the south were already being converted to Islam.

About a century later, with the sanction of the papacy, the most powerful monarch of Europe engaged in voyages of discovery and colonization. The papal bull of Pope Alexander VI divided the world into halves, one each for the Iberian Catholic monarchies: Spain and Portugal.[18] The Philippine Islands fell in the Portuguese half, but because of inexact geographical knowledge, Spain laid claim to the Philippines when Fernao Magalhaes, more popularly known as Ferdinand Magellan, the first European to achieve the circumnavigation of the world, landed there on March 17, 1521. Ironically, Fernao Magalhaes was a Portuguese in the service of the Spanish king. Magalhaes was welcomed by the leader of the big island of Cebu but repelled by the chief of the small island of Mactan. When Magalhaes attacked Mactan to subjugate its chief, Lapulapu, however, the Portuguese captain was killed in the battle.

Later voyages of the Spanish sought to establish a permanent colony. A Spanish captain, Ruy Lopez de Villalobos, named one of the islands "Filipinas," in honor of King Felipe II. The name was later taken for the entire archipelago. In 1571, an expedition led by Miguel Lopez de Legazpi established a Spanish colony in what is now Manila. With the help of some groups of Filipinos, he embarked on the conquest of the islands, a process that took hundreds of years.

During three centuries of Spanish imperialism, the whole archipelago was never placed under effective control by the Spaniards. Far fewer Spanish soldiers and settlers went to Asia than went to the Americas. The conquest of Mexico and Peru was destructive. It introduced diseases like small pox and syphilis, to which the Indians were not immune. With more sophisticated armaments, in a generation or so the Spaniards imposed their language and culture and brought about the mixture of races in what is now called Latin America. They were less successful in the Philippines.[19] The friar was usually the only white man in a Filipino village. He was the religious and secular head, the confessor, and the representative of the king in the town. Because of his wide-ranging duties and scope of authority, he was prone to commit abuses, and he did.

The head of the colony was the governor-general. His complete title was *"gobernador y capitan general y vice-real patron."* As governor-general, he governed for the king of Spain; he headed the colonial government and was the chief legislator. As captain-general, he was the head of all armed forces; and as vice-royal patron, he represented the king as patron of the Catholic Church.[20] In his last role, he often clashed with church leaders.

This elevated office, which is filled by a lieutenant general of the National Armies, is vested with extraordinary and the most important attributes. . . . Annexed to this office are those of Vice-Royal Patron of the Indias, Captain-General-in-Chief of the Army of Filipinas, Inspector General of all troops and institutions, Supreme Chief of Naval Forces, and President of all Corporations and Associations of an official character.[21]

His authoritarian rule was basically unchecked, except by the friars and the members of the priestly orders.

The imposition of Spanish rule was made possible by a policy of *"divide et impera,"* "divide and rule." Dividing the Philippine peoples was easy because in the first place, they had never been unified by a central authority and were divided into many ethnolinguistic groups. There was no central government either. The Spaniards capitalized on internal feuds among the groups and used one to conquer another. In collaboration with the native leaders and with their armies, territories were declared under the sovereign rule of the Spanish monarch. To make efficient their quest for "god, gold, and glory," the Spaniards brought together the Filipinos from their scattered dwellings into *reducciones*, within hearing of church bells (*"bajo de la campana"*).[22] Proximity facilitated control, tribute collection, conversion, and the practice of Christianity as well as the enforcement of other impositions such as forced labor and government monopolies. The Spanish king granted *encomiendas*, lists of names for the purpose and privilege of collecting tributes, to Spanish military leaders and to other grantees, called *encomenderos*, in exchange for their services in the conquest. Filipinos who collaborated with the Spaniards often performed the task of tribute collection and were granted privileges and formal authority over others.[23]

The Spaniards granted those Filipinos *principalia* status, and over generations, they exercised their influence and power. They served as intermediaries to the Spanish conquerors. From among the *principalia, gobernadorcillos* were selected or chosen by lot. The town (*pueblo*) therefore was governed by the *principalia* with the strong influence of the parish priest. Provinces, which are groups of towns or municipalities, were in turn governed by *alcaldes-mayores* or governors. An *alcalde* was the political and military chief, magistrate, and delegate of the treasury. The position of *alcalde* was considered lucrative in the Spanish colonies and appointments to "alcaldeships" were bought. The investment reaped many rewards with the privilege of conducting and controlling business in the province. The *alcalde* was also allotted a percentage of the tributes collected. Collecting more than was required by law was a widespread practice because of increased bonuses. The Spanish crown required *alcaldes* to post bonds and securities and to submit an inventory of their estates. The *alcaldes* were also subject to audit; in addition, they might be required to pay fines for excesses, but their profits always exceeded their investments, and none of the safeguards deterred corruption.[24]

By its very nature, colonialism adversely affects the colonized. Spanish colonialism was no exception. Food became scarce because farmers were taken from their farms to do forced labor such as building ships. The dependent and unproductive population increased and, with it, the demand for food. Scarcities produced increases in the prices of commodities.[25] The transition to a monetized economy was painful for the natives.

The Philippines functioned as an entrepot during the galleon trade when China sold a vast array of commodities in exchange for silver and gold mined in the Spanish colonies in America. Ships for that trade were built and maintained by Filipinos. They were served by Filipino crews as well. Some speculators in the trade even got their capital from profits accrued in the Philippines.[26] The colonial government established monopolies in which the kinds and quantities of crops to be planted were dictated. The sale of crops was limited to the government or its agents, and at their prescribed prices. Control was also imposed on processing and storage.[27] That control was called *vandala*, by which governors had monopolies of trade within their jurisdiction. They bought goods from Manila with their capital usually taken from loans, and then sold them to the natives. In turn, the latter sold their products to the governor. The prices in both transactions were dictated by the governor.[28] Land accumulated in the hands of friar corporations and government officials. With the introduction of ownership through written titles and legal documents, the natives were cheated by those who controlled the bureaucracy.[29] Government was rife with corruption. A government position became an opportunity to exploit land, human energy, and labor, as well as to enjoy perquisites and privileges.

During the middle of the eighteenth century, the transformation of the Philippine economy began. No longer was economic activity focused on the galleon trade. The accumulation of land, in the hands of friar corporations and Spaniards, brought about the *hacienda* or plantation system. Large tracts of land were exploited for cash crops such as tobacco, sugar, and abaca. The abandonment of rice lands for the planting of other agricultural commodities for export earnings resulted in rice shortages, so rice had to be imported from other Asian countries.

When the last of the Manila galleons sailed in 1813 and when the Real Compania de Filipinas was abolished in 1834, more foreign ships and traders entered the archipelago. Manila was opened as an international port together with Iloilo, Cebu, and Sual. The British and the Americans became the Philippines' largest trading partners. As in British India, imported textiles, which were cheaper, replaced the locally woven cloth for consumption. By the end of the nineteenth century, a great number of foreign firms were booming in the Philippines, processing and exporting Philippine agricultural produce to the world; thus developed the popularity of Manila paper, Manila hemp, and Philippine cigars.[30]

The economic transformation, as well as the establishment of direct links with Europe through the opening of the Suez Canal in 1869, made possible the influx of

European liberalism. The ripple effects of Spanish liberalism and reformism, a latecomer compared to its European counterparts, influenced the Philippines. The wealthy class of landowners and traders created by the economic boom gained access to education. Enlightened ideas led to demands for reform, which were considered subversive and revolutionary by conservative rulers. To the friars, reformism was heresy and a threat to their dominance.

NATIONALISM AND REVOLUTION

Hundreds of revolts were staged against Spanish abuses throughout the 300 years of Spanish rule;[31] however, the revolts were separate and local. The coming of liberal ideas and the grievances resulting from racial discrimination coalesced with the collective suffering and frustration brought about by colonialism. Racial tensions existed among native Filipinos, called *indios*; those Spaniards born in the Philippines, called *insulares*; those Spaniards born in Spain, called *peninsulares*; and those of mixed races, the Spanish and Chinese *mestizos*.[32] Racial conflicts were carried into the church, as seen in the discrimination against native and mestizo members of the clergy. Liberal ideas acquired by mestizos influenced and inspired them to plead for and demand reforms, but because of their race, the elite created by economic wealth did not have political authority. They clamored for increased political participation, which meant participation in the affairs of the colonies. Filipino students in Spain and other countries of Europe published newspapers and leaflets asking for reform in the colonies.[33] Among the leaders of the propaganda movement was the Philippine national hero, Jose Rizal. In his two novels, *Noli Me Tangere* and *El Filibusterismo*, both written in Spanish, he described a cancerous society in Noli and a revolution that failed in Fili.[34]

The writings of propagandists influenced the beginnings of a movement toward an armed revolution. Andres Bonifacio, a warehouseman, organized the secret society that launched the revolution, but its existence was divulged to the friars.[35] Rizal, meanwhile, earned the ire of the Spanish authorities for inspiring an armed struggle he himself did not condone. As a result, he was executed in 1896. The revolution was riven by factionalism, division, and ethnic rivalries. Andres Bonifacio, the father of the revolution, was even executed by other rebels for alleged treason. Emilio Aguinaldo, the emergent military leader from Cavite, consolidated his leadership in the revolutionary army. A truce ended the battles; however, even while the "Te Deum" was being sung in the Manila cathedral to celebrate the truce and even though revolutionary leaders had gone into self-exile in Hong Kong, the fighting continued between the belligerents. Both sides broke their promises. The Spaniards continued their repressive policies and did not pay full indemnity to the Filipino rebels. The rebels did not surrender all armaments and deposited the indemnity as downpayment for arms and ammunitions. During their Hong Kong exile, self-exiled leaders bought arms with the money from the armistice and unofficially communicated with American representatives in Asia.[36]

THE BEGINNINGS OF AMERICAN INVOLVEMENT

After the settlement of the western frontier, the United States directed its attention toward the Pacific and Asia. Commodore Matthew Perry forced the opening of Japan from its many years of seclusion and isolation. Even though they were latecomers in the scramble for colonies, the Americans conducted brisk trade in Asia, including the Philippines. The possibilities of a foothold in the rich market of Asia and a "chunk of the Chinese melon" were a welcome prospect, so the U.S. government proposed an "open door policy" for China.

As early as the 1790s, an American ship unloaded cargo in the Philippines and took back exports such as sugar, hemp, and indigo. When the Philippines was opened to international trade, U.S. commerce increased. Two businesses—Russell, Sturgis, and Company; and Peele, Hubbell, and Company—engaged in various enterprises: banking, insurance, trade, and shipping. In the 1850s, American vessels entering and leaving the port of Manila carried the highest tonnage. Between 1880 and 1889, the United States was the chief importer of Philippine products and U.S. trade accounted for "39 percent of the total annual average value of all Philippine exports, buying 59 percent of all sugar and 44 percent of all hemp exported."[37] Even before the sugar quota, the Philippines had been a source for sweetening American coffee and candies.

The mysterious sinking of the ship U.S.S. *Maine* in the harbor of Havana, Cuba in 1898 raised American patriotic feelings and initiated the march toward the Spanish-American War. Theodore Roosevelt, an ardent imperialist and Assistant Secretary of the Navy at the time, ordered Commodore George Dewey to sail his squadron to Manila Bay. The Spanish navy under the command of Admiral Patricio Montojo neither wanted to hurt Spanish pride nor surrender without honor. In a mock battle between the decrepit Spanish armada and the American navy, the Americans proclaimed victory, and Intramuros, the Spanish "walled city" of Manila, was surrendered to the Americans. That mock battle brought to American attention the existence of the Philippine Islands.[38] The Treaty of Paris of 1898, which concluded the Spanish-American War, ceded the Philippines, Cuba, and other Spanish colonies to the United States for $60 million.

The Filipinos, in the meantime, resumed their struggle for independence. They were already in control of areas outside Manila during the Battle of Manila Bay. Revolutionary leaders who returned from self-exile brought back arms and ammunitions. With the massive support of the populace, they scored successes in the armed struggle that culminated in the declaration of Philippine independence on June 12, 1898. The Filipinos organized a government of their own, wrote their constitution, and established a government with a president, a congress, and a judiciary. While that government already existed in fact,[39] Americans were heatedly debating the morality of imperialism. President William McKinley, before a Methodist group, said that on bended knees he prayed to God and realized that the United States through "benevolent assimilation" should take the islands in order "to civilize and Christianize" them. Little did he know that hundreds of years before, friars had introduced Christianity to the islanders whom some Americans perceived as barbarians.[40]

"Civilize Them with a Krag" was the song of the soldiers who came to impose American rule.[41] The Philippine-American War caused an inordinate amount of dislocation, devastation, and suffering. Torture, massacres, and pillaging occurred. With its similarities to the Vietnam War, the Philippine-American War is sometimes referred to as the "first Vietnam." The war, in American history books officially called the Philippine insurrection, lasted from 1899 to 1901, at which time a civil government was organized.[42] Those who continued to resist were called bandits and brigands. Similar to those Filipinos who helped the Spaniards, collaborators cooperated with the new colonizers, once again facilitating the coming of the second wave of colonialists.[43] Although severely restricted, nationalist expression remained. The display of the Philippine flag was banned and advocacy of independence was prohibited during the first years of American occupation, but through theater and music, anti-American feelings were expressed.[44]

The Americans established a civilian bureaucracy as a response to those reform-minded Filipino elites who wished to participate in government. Their participation dampened nationalist aspirations, and politicians settled for the political power granted then under U.S. rule. Electoral politics was implemented, and political parties were allowed to be organized. In the beginning, there was a Partido Federalista, which aimed at the incorporation of the Philippines into the American Union; however, the party did not gain enough following and was short-lived, whereas the parties who played independence politics survived. All political parties claimed in their public pronouncements that they were for independence while in private some of them seriously feared losing the privileges and advantages they enjoyed with the Philippines as an American colony.[45]

Filipino participation in governance increased gradually. In 1907 was elected a legislature composed of Filipinos, which served as the lower house. In 1916, the Jones Law provided for a bicameral legislature, with a senate and a house of representatives composed of Filipinos. The courts were also Filipinized; in fact, the Supreme Court of the Philippines was the first branch of government to have a Filipino majority. The Philippines was governed by a governor-general whose vice-governor also occupied the position of secretary of public instruction, a department considered pivotal in the American colonial set up. Before 1916, the Speaker of the Assembly was considered the focus of authority among Filipino politicians. During the Jones Law period, the president of the Senate was the center of power and influence. Manuel L. Quezon, the first Senate president, later became the first president of the Philippine Commonwealth.[46]

The quest for independence culminated in a commonwealth government inaugurated in 1935 and intended to preside over a ten-year transition toward self-rule, a government for which foreign affairs and defense were to be handled by the United States; however, a Filipino president and legislature were to be elected to assume the functions of government. After more than three decades of colonization, when the commonwealth government was proclaimed, the United States had already significantly affected Philippine political, cultural, and economic life. The Americans established a public system of education and taught the English language. They improved public services and public health but maintained the system of land tenancy.

A system of electoral democracy was introduced to facilitate the elite's co-opting power and to cater to their reformist demands. Robert Pringle, a former U.S. Foreign Service officer in the Philippines, asserted that the creation of American democracy and its assumed benevolence were myths of Philippine-U.S. relations. According to Pringle:

Myth number one is that we created democracy in the Philippines; that our colonialism was more enlightened than European colonialism, both in its motivations and its consequences. In fact, American rule bolstered a preexisting landed elite, encouraging it to express itself through representative forms. The result was perhaps as "democratic" as Mississippi in 1900. The forms were there but the substance was *sui generis*. Myth number two is that Filipino political leaders struggled for their independence and that we graciously acceded, extending it to them short of revolution, thereby confirming our superiority to other colonists. In fact . . . , we decided for reasons of self interest to divest ourselves of the Philippines before local leaders wanted full independence, under conditions (world depression and looming war) which bid fair to destroy the Philippine nation, and nearly did.[47]

When "popular" elections were introduced, those qualified to vote had to be male, had to be at least twenty-three years old, had to have held a municipal office before August 13, 1898, had to be literate in either English or Spanish, and had either to have owned real property valued at at least $230 or to have paid an annual tax of $15. The qualifications were formulated by the Taft Commission upon the recommendation of Filipinos whom they consulted and who, as it turned out, wanted stricter qualifications for greater exclusivity.[48] The elite thus gained the most from the system and "were definitely recognized as the governing class."[49] According to O. D. Corpuz, only 3% of the national population comprised the electorate, so "the growth and continuing hegemony of the great local family dynasties in Filipino politics" was made possible.[50] The *principalia* of the Spanish period mediated between the masses and the new colonizers. They performed the same role in a different regime. The Americans needed them to impose order and leadership and to pacify the population. Historians of the era referred to the American colonial period as "*compadre* colonialism" during which period the Filipino elite became *compadres*, or close friends, of American governors, thereby establishing a network of alliances among themselves. According to Peter W. Stanley:

There was a hidden price for all this. America's reliance upon collaboration and suasion to maintain its insular empire made the collaborators a privileged group. Positioning themselves between the two real loci of power and authority in the islands, the American government and the mass of the Filipino people, they became indispensable mediators. Since the only credible collaborators (the only people with the authority, outlook, and education necessary both to deal with Americans and to deliver the allegiance of the people) were the members of the established elite the imperialism of suasion thus became a bulwark of class interest.[51]

The Filipino elite continued to solidify position and power through collaboration with the American colonizers. "Free trade" with the United States created a dependent Filipino economy. The Tariff Acts of 1909 and 1919 increased the volume of trade between the colonizer and the colonized. A flood of imported, mass-produced, American goods discouraged domestic industrialization and greater economic diversification. The Philippines continued to be an exporter of a few agricultural products and raw materials, such as abaca, coconut, sugar, and tobacco, the market for which was pegged for the United States. Economic dependency on the United States shaped the Filipino taste for the consumption of material goods. That taste was referred to as colonial mentality; current observers call it "hamburgerization."[52]

The life of the commonwealth government was interrupted by the Japanese invasion.[53] Japan's militarism grew in the 1930s, as did its desperate need for natural resources to supply its burgeoning industrialization. Having limited territory and natural resources but unlimited energy and will, the Japanese desired to achieve true imperial status by establishing a Greater East Asia Co-Prosperity Sphere. It promised peace, prosperity, and independence to other Asian countries. Japan succeeded in rousing nationalist and anti-western feelings among other Asians; however, they did not succeed with the Filipinos. The Americans had already promised the Filipinos political independence and had granted relative freedom compared to Japanese control. American cruelty during the Philippine-American War had been forgotten. Now Filipinos were fighting with Americans and supporting them against the Japanese. Further sentimental ties between Filipinos and Americans were forged during the World War II. The Filipinos looked at the Americans with "*utang na loob*" or a "debt of gratitude." General Douglas MacArthur was welcomed as a folk hero because he fulfilled his promise to the Philippines.[54]

On July 4, 1946, the Philippines regained its political independence. Aided by the sentimentality produced by the war and the forgotten ill-feelings of the brutal conquest, the Filipinos allowed sets of impositions to be added to their constitution. Those impositions, couched in friendly terms, were labeled as "special," but others termed them "neocolonial." To high American officials, the Philippines was a loose friend and ally; to others, the Philippines was an American satellite.[55]

Devastated by war and needing major rehabilitation, the government of the Philippines amended the Philippine Constitution granting equal rights to Americans in the exploitation and use of natural resources. No individual claim in excess of $500 would be granted to the Philippines as provided for in the Philippine Rehabilitation Act of 1946 unless an executive agreement had been reached between the Philippines and the United States, giving American citizens parity rights.[56] Free trade between the two countries was also provided; unlimited U.S. exports could enter the Philippines duty-free for eight years. The same privilege was granted to Philippine exports to the U.S., albeit with significant exceptions: cigars, coconut oil, cordage, buttons of pearl, sugar, and scrap tobacco. Those exports, which are the Philippines' main exports, were subject to quotas in order to protect the American domestic market.[57]

Also forged in 1947 was an agreement giving the United States free use of twenty-three military installations and bases for ninety-nine years and access to skilled English-speaking Filipino workers. A mutual-defense treaty was signed in 1951, whereby the parties agreed to "separately and jointly by self-help and mutual aid maintain and develop their individual and collective capacity to resist armed attack."[58]

After independence, Philippine foreign policy assumed a mutuality of interest with the United States. As enunciated by Manuel Roxas, the first president of the Philippine Republic, unconditional cooperation with the United States was a pillar of Philippine foreign policy. Whatever the U.S. stand in foreign policy and however the country voted in the United Nations, the Philippines followed suit.[59]

Following the example of the McCarthy witch hunt, the Committee of Anti-Filipino Activities, similar to the Committee on Un-American Activities, was established in the Philippine Congress. The Joint United States Military Advisory Group (JUSMAG), composed of U.S. advisers to the Philippine armed forces, was established. It immensely influenced the tactics and operations of the Armed Forces of the Philippines (AFP), including training in counterinsurgency. The Central Intelligence Agency (CIA), in one of its most victorious battles against local insurgency, made possible the success story of the popular Philippine president Ramon Magsaysay and his campaign to quell the Huk rebellion. Counterinsurgency measures that were tested in putting down the Huk rebellion were again used by Col. Edward Lansdale and company in Vietnam.[60]

The structure of the government provided for in the Philippine Constitution was almost a carbon copy of its American model. It established a presidential form of government with three branches: the executive, the legislative vested in a bicameral congress with a senate and a house of representatives, and the judiciary vested in a supreme court. Before the imposition of martial law in 1972, Philippine politics was participative. Elections were held every two years, alternating between national and local elections, but it was an imperfect democracy where access to power was usually based on wealth. People tended to vote on personalities, group loyalties, and social relationships rather than on issues. The party system was called "one-and-a-half" because there was no substantial difference between the two major parties.[61] They both functioned as a mechanism for gaining control of public office as well as patronage. Nepotism and influence peddling were prominent. Rampant graft and corruption were the never-ending political issues in elections where candidates denounced one another for alleged wrongdoings, but the system withstood open and free discussion and criticism. No president was reelected except Ferdinand Marcos. The media, the "freest in the world,"[62] carried stories of political scandals and revealed congressional investigations in progress and inquiries into irregular government activities. Politics was sometimes called the national sport of the Filipinos because they had as great a passion for it as Americans have for football and baseball.

The military was clearly subordinated to civilian authority. Promotions and appointments as well as the budget for national defense had to pass through the Philippine Congress. The subordination effectively checked the military. (Indeed, even teachers enjoyed greater prestige and status than did army officers. Education held a higher priority in the national budget than did the military.)

Crime was rampant, and rural unrest, inspired by the unjust system of land tenure and abuse of tenants by landowners, was prominent. Law and order were disturbed by political lords and their "goons," and by big landowners and their bodyguards fighting to protect their wealth and power. The government's inability to improve social justice and the oppressive gap between the rich and the poor led to the clamor for social reforms. In the late 1960s, students, workers, and other citizens increasingly expressed their demands for reform in the "parliament of the streets."

POLITICS AND SOCIAL VALUES

In a dependent and underdeveloped economy, certain social values are reinforced. Central to the Philippine value system is reciprocity or *utang na loob*—the exchange of services and goods between individuals belonging to two different groups. That reciprocity permeates transactions between individuals, social classes, and ethnic groups. The fulfillment of social contracts of exchange guarantees smooth relationships or *pakikisama* ("to be with someone or with a group"); in contrast, a breach of that reciprocity would cause *hiya*—shame, loss of face, embarrassment, or the "uncomfortable feeling that accompanies awareness of being in a socially unacceptable position, or performing a socially unacceptable action."[63] Social acceptance, as well as the sense of belonging, is important to the pursuit of economic security and to social mobility, basic aspirations of a Filipino. In striving to earn a living and achieve upward mobility, Filipinos must conform to the unwritten rules of contractual exchange in order to gain what is considered success as well as to earn social acceptance. One must have access to and be part of a network of relationships of established exchanges. Philippine society is composed of what anthropologists call "dyadic alliances" extending across boundaries of economic group and class.[64] According to Lande:

The stress upon particular goals fosters the formation of alliances extending across boundaries of economic group and class. This is so because when individuals' interests are advanced through the seeking of special favors, the role of dispenser of favors becomes a very strategic one. Aware of this fact, those fortunate enough to occupy such a role learn to extract, as a quid pro quo, equivalent rewards from those whom they favor. Mutually pleasing transactions of this sort tend to be repeated. Thus are established fairly stable mutual aid arrangements between pairs of individuals under which each partner helps the other pursue his personal goals.[65]

The dominant party is the patron, whereas the subordinate is the client. In a national network one is both a client and a patron depending on the level of power and authority, wealth, professional access to government services, and other possible gains for reward and prestige. Those directly linked in the network are close to one another and have face-to-face relationships. In the Philippines and other traditional societies throughout the world, patron status is correlated with land ownership.[66] The laborers and tenants are tied to the *inquilino* (subleasees); the *inquilinos*, in turn, are linked to *hacienderos* (landowners). In modernizing societies, new brokers and patrons are created. With the centralization of the nation-state, the monetization and linking of markets and local economies, government officials, businesspeople and traders become part of the new pool of patrons. They are linked together by bureaucracy and markets usually located in the capital city. Their network permeates society. Politics is conducted through the relationships of patrons and clients.

Local organizations and associations, be they civic, religious, or political, draw members not so much because of the groups' manifest goals but because of "common interest in structuring power relationship along particular lines."[67] Vertical and horizontal alliances coalesce behind a leader who personifies the organization. Leadership is personalistic; it is advanced through relationships with the supporters. When the allies of a leader are dissatisfied with the organization or are not given equal dominance or concessions, they attract followers through some promise or reward and establish a faction or another organization. Factional rivalries are not uncommon.

Leaders of rival alliances were recruited by the two political parties. The alliances were in turn the foundation of the two-party system. Since they were not founded on ideological and programmatic or policy differences, the two parties did not differ from each other; they offered no clear platforms. Campaigns for office were based on criticizing opponents and highlighting their wrongdoings. Parties did not have card-carrying members. The party system was characterized as a "cadre" rather than a "mass" party.[68] In mass parties, rules and regulations govern membership. Members perform duties and pay dues. The party enforces discipline, and the members join the party because of their belief in its goals and programs. They are also attached to party symbols and ideology. To the contrary, membership in Philippine political parties was amorphous. Members could be called not "members" but more properly "supporters." They supported a party in relation to their immediate leaders' connections. Campaign funds were raised through business connections and supporters such as big landowners and local leaders, not through the mass membership.

The electorate consisted of a mass of voters uncommitted to parties and of loyalists to favorite candidates or personalities. For a member of a political party to vote for the candidate of the other party would not be unusual. Some leaders of one party even vied for office through the opposing party as "guest candidates." Turncoatism was common. According to one sociologist, "The Filipino votes for the sure winner."[69] The *liders*[70] sided with the winning group to assure themselves of a good reward for their effort and investment. The rewards or patronage accrued not only to them but also to their allies. It was important to be a *segurista*—one who makes certain of the results of one's actions.[71] After elections, supporters collected the patronage due them. Campaigns were based on promises for employment or the release of pork barrel funds by the incumbents, so supporters made sure that promises were kept and funds for projects were released.

Mary Racelis Hollnsteiner's classic study of local politics described the outcome of municipal elections thus:

Victory with no patronage prospects is at best hollow. . . . The aftermath of election time is a period of joys and disappointments depending on whose side one was on. The defeated partymen analyze voting records and seek reasons for their loss. Supporters of the victorious party are now *utang na loob* creditors and proceed to collect their due through seeking job appointments or recommendations for jobs. The entrepreneurs and *baklad* fishermen who voted for the winning party especially those who actively campaigned for the victorious candidates can now relax as they know that failure to pay their taxes will not initiate any punitive action on the part of the municipal administration. They will be conveniently forgotten while some of their competitors who chose unwisely may be harassed for non-payment of taxes.[72]

The most influential leaders of the system, therefore, are those who are able to use the patron-client network. In a province, the leader is the person who has access to land, employment, privileges, services, and further connections. The master politician in that system is the one most able to mediate and adjudicate among competing alliances, form bigger coalitions of supporters and assure the continuance of the system, preside over the system of rewards and punishment, and manage a network of dyadic alliances starting from the smallest village to the national government. This individual manipulates symbols and engages in rhetoric for public consumption, a rhetoric behind which he maneuvers for guaranteed advantage over others. Such a political system, therefore, has an inherently conservative character. In a society with a skewed economic distribution, social classes and groups who have distinct advantage over others in terms of wealth and influence have a vested interest in preserving their gains and expanding them. They often distribute rewards that are minimal in comparison with the return. Those who have less are dependent on those who have more; as a result, superior-subordinate relationships are continued and perpetuated and reciprocity is valued. Loyalty to the "contractual obligations" incurred is also perpetuated. Economic dependency feeds on the value system and vice versa. Thus, the introduction of programmatic and policy changes comes excruciatingly slowly; further, substantive change meets extreme resistance, as exemplified by the legislation and policy on land reform and the issue of land ownership and tenancy. The abolition of tenancy and the distribution of ownership of land had been popular campaign rhetoric. No radical change took place in spite of enactments of land reform and the declaration of the abolition of tenancy because most political leaders themselves had power and wealth based on land.[73]

Campaign slogans take the place of policies. Vote buying and bribery were rampant and worked effectively during elections. Promises of favors abounded. Pecuniary benefits were enough to induce desired behavior. In an economy of scarcity, the utmost concern is survival. According to Philippine political scientist Remigio E. Agpalo, "The *tao*, thinking first and foremost of the survival of himself and his family, is little interested in high-sounding policies, ideologies or principles of good government and administration. What interests him is which party, group or person will give him a job."[74] *Pulitika* (politics) is, however, perceived negatively by the people as nothing more than jockeying for positions and grabbing power.[75]

Opposition politics often meant criticizing the incumbent for abuse of authority and the use of public office for personal and family advantage; however, citizens implicitly expected public office to be used for private gain because they expected patronage from their leaders.

The value system guarantees the continuity of the economic and social structure. There have always been forces for change, such as nationalism and ideology, albeit they have been too weak to cause change in the economy and culture. The history of the Philippines from colonial times to the present has seen the integration of that value system. Rather than being an aberration, an authoritarian system represents the peak of the system's evolution.

THE RISE OF MARCOS

In 1965, while nationalist and reformist rallies and demonstrations were beginning to gain momentum, political parties were gearing up for the presidential election. By the third year of his presidency, Diosdado Macapagal was already a lame-duck president. He devoted the whole year to visiting remote areas to win support for the November election as well as to show that he was concerned about the common person.

The truth of the one-and-a-half party system was again to become apparent in that election. The Liberal and Nacionalista Parties consisted of coteries of politicians connected by patronage from the national government to the ranks in the provinces, cities, and municipalities, down to the smallest *barrios* (neighborhoods). For convenience and for personal and political advantages, turncoatism was common.

Before independence, Manuel L. Quezon was the reigning politico: president of the Commonwealth government and the Nacionalista Party. The Philippines' first authoritarian, he considered his opponents to be merely "barking at the moon" when expressing views contrary to his. Until his death in the United States, where the Philippine government was exiled during World War II, he was the most influential Filipino politician. After the war, when the Philippines was due its independence from the United States, Sergio Osmeña, Quezon's vice-president, briefly succeeded the presidency. To be able to confront Osmeña political objectives in the presidential election, Roxas left the Nacionalistas to organize the Liberal Party. The Philippines henceforth had the Liberal and Nacionalista Parties, neither of which was liberal or nationalist, respectively. Politicians who revolted against Osmeña moved to Roxas's camp with the thought that his popularity would surely bring them to power. Roxas won the election and became the first president of the independent Philippine Republic.[76]

The third president of the Republic was the charismatic Ramon Magsaysay. He rose to prominence as the secretary of national defense to President Elpidio Quirino. In the American-assisted counterinsurgency operations, Magsaysay won the affection of both Americans and Filipinos as a popular leader who could match Quirino. There was widespread dissatisfaction with the Quirino administration's corruption. Magsaysay resigned from the cabinet before the 1953 presidential election, and, having gained patrons from the Nacionalista Party, moved to its banners and became its official candidate. Magsaysay thereby captured the presidency.[77]

In 1965, another turncoat was about to become president. Ferdinand Marcos, the Senate president and president himself of the Liberal Party, had ambitions for the presidency. His only hope for challenging the incumbent Diosdado Macapagal, another Liberal, was to move to the Nacionalista camp. In an adroit move, the president of the Liberal Party switched party cards and maneuvered to win the nomination for the Nacionalista candidacy.

The 1965 campaign was furiously waged. Both candidates visited the many islands of the Philippines and shook hands with the farmers, fishermen, and workers. Ferdinand Marcos, a politician from Ilocos Norte, a northern Luzon province, hoped to garner most of the votes in his area. His wife, Imelda Romualdez-Marcos, and vice-presidential candidate Fernando Lopez, gathered popularity for him in the southern province. Lopez also brought with him the wealth and influence of a southern clan whose business empire included interests in agriculture and the mass media.

Who was Ferdinand Marcos?[78] Marcos was born in Batac, Ilocos Norte, to Mariano Marcos and Josefa Edralin. The Marcoses and the Edralins were minor families in local politics. During the American era, Mariano Marcos was a one-time assemblyman in the National Assembly. Josefa Edralin was a schoolteacher. Marcos studied in Manila and pursued law at the University of the Philippines College of Law. During his senior year, Marcos was brought to court. Two days after the electoral defeat of his father, the winner in the election, Julio Nalundasan, while brushing his teeth near a window in his house, was killed by an assassin's bullet. Marcos was a marksman and trained in firearms. With the defeat of his father and because of his marksmanship, Marcos became a suspect in the assassination. Vengeance was considered a possible motive for the crime. Marcos defended himself in court, but the Court of First Instance pronounced him guilty of the crime. While in prison, he reviewed for the bar examination. In addition to graduating with honors in his law class, Marcos topped the bar, earning admirers and sympathizers—in the Philippines, placing first in the bar is a national honor. With his success, the Supreme Court reversed the lower court's decision and acquitted Marcos of the crime.

During the war, Marcos served as a guerrilla, but his war exploits were later overblown and again used to put him in the limelight, winning him more support than he deserved. He had been awarded medals of recognition right after the war, but twenty years later he became the most decorated hero of the Philippines, eclipsing even the most recognized leaders of the resistance against the Japanese. It was contended that he received some nine medals in one day in 1963 from the president in order to dissuade him from running for the presidency himself.[79]

One day in 1955, while Congress was in session, Marcos's attention was caught by a beautiful young woman in the gallery. Imelda Romualdez was a chaperon to her cousin. She was the niece of then speaker of the House Congressman Daniel Z. Romualdez. In May 1955, the eleven-day courtship ended in marriage before Judge Francisco Ma. Chanco of La Trinidad Valley in Benguet. Later, Marcos converted to Roman Catholicism to receive the benefit of a church wedding. (He had been born and baptized in the Aglipayan or Philippine Independent Church.) In the context of

Philippine marriages, the Marcos-Romualdez marriage meant the union of two families. The Romualdezes were prominent in Visayas, but the family originated in Manila. Supreme Court Justice Norberto Romualdez came from the same Romualdez clan as the Speaker of the House Daniel Romualdez. Imelda, however, came from a less prominent branch of the family.[80]

During the election, Marcos gained the support of both his and Imelda's home provinces. Fernando Lopez, a senator from Iloilo and a former vice-president to Quirino, brought the financial and business conglomerate backing and more of the southern vote to the ticket. Prominent in business, the Lopez family owned vast plantations of sugar, the primary export of the Philippines. The family's interests included newspapers, radio and television stations, and the Manila Electric Company, the largest electric power franchise in the Philippines.

Charges of graft and corruption were hurled right and left. In politics still devoid of an ideology and a clear government platform, politicians resorted to denunciations and allegations of graft and corruption. Mistakes buried in the past were brought back to life. Personalities were overly praised and possible scandals were dug up. Past favors were reckoned with and political dues collected. Promises of future employment or concessions were made in exchange for votes. Following the Philippine tradition of not reelecting an incumbent president, the Marcos-Lopez ticket won with the majority vote. Marcos's slogan, "This nation can be great again," may have rung a bell with the electorate, or his "messianic belief of himself and his destiny not only developed his charisma in attracting the electorate, it [may] also [have] enabled him to twist the interpretation of events to fit his own concepts" and political objectives.[81] During his first term as president, Marcos considerably strengthened the powers and resources of the military and civilian bureaucracies and put them at his disposal.

As the 1969 presidential elections approached, Marcos mustered those political resources to win reelection. Based on the 1935 Constitution, if reelected, Marcos's second term would be his last term in office and thus his last chance for the presidency. His first term had scarcely begun when he hinted at revising the presidential tenure of office.[82] During the midterm election in 1967, six Nacionalistas gained Senate seats out of eight vacancies. A majority of the Nacionalistas were also elected into the House of Representatives. The gain brought a fellow Nacionalista, Jose B. Laurel, to the speakership of the House.

It was also during that election that the young governor of Tarlac, Benigno S. Aquino, Jr. of the Liberal Party, topped the senatorial slate of eight nationally elected senators. The Philippine Senate was composed of twenty-four senators each with a six-year term. A rotation of elections held every two years replaced eight members.[83] The election of Aquino to the Senate gave the opposition to Marcos considerable strength. Aquino was an ardent and articulate critic of the administration.[84]

In 1968, Aquino wrote an article in *Foreign Affairs* that was a summary of issues and problems which confronted Philippine society.[85] According to Aquino in "What's Wrong with the Philippines," the country had a government that was almost bankrupt, state agencies ridden by debts and honeycombed with graft, industries in pathetic distress, prices in a continuing spiral, and Filipinos feeling sapped of confidence, hope, and will.

In 1967-68, the Philippines was plagued with an economic crisis involving an outflow of capital, an imbalance of trade, a rise in imports coupled with the decline of exports, an increase in smuggling, and a decrease in industrial growth. The Philippines was not able to meet its sugar quota for the United States, raising doubts about whether the government would be able to meet commitments in subsequent years and threatening a cutback in the quota.[86] Monetary factors such as the dollar exchange and central bank credit restrictions also aggravated the crisis. The peso slowly sank in value, and a foreign exchange surplus was created only because the U.S. government spent money in the Philippines.[87]

The Philippine government hoped that a policy of encouraging foreign investment would work, and so enacted the Investment Incentives Law in 1967. It placed a ceiling of 40% on Philippine equity for corporations. It allowed an equity of over 40% as long as Philippine nationals did not buy shares offered after the eleventh year of registration with the Board of Investments (BOI). It also guaranteed property rights and nonexpropriation to foreign investors.[88]

In 1969, the BOI started giving aid to 107 preferred and pioneering projects, totaling 1.7 billion pesos in investment, of which 1.10 billion pesos would go to manufacturing, 444.2 million pesos to mining, and 154.2 million pesos to agriculture.[89] At the same time, the Marcos administration overspent millions of pesos to boost its image and assure reelection. Marcos even hired American political consultants and strategists.

Specialized budgets, pork-barrel funds, and even departmental budgetary allocations were used for what was called the most expensive election in the Philippines.[90] It was a "campaign overkill." The president distributed 4,000 pesos each to all barrio captains, who were the leaders of Philippine villages or barrios, which are the smallest political units of local government. Patronage politics was oiled in order to assure grass-roots support; furthermore, Marcos subsidized his political allies in their individual campaigns for Senaterial and House seats.[91]

The opposition's inability to produce a viable candidate became an advantage for Marcos. Possible candidates were Cornelio Villareal, the former Speaker of the House, Senators Gerado Roxas, Jovito Salonga, and Jose Diokno. Neither Villareal nor Diokno had a national following at the time. Roxas and Salonga were brought to national attention in the 1965 election "but neither had substantial organizations" yet.[92] Both were also considered too young, as was Aquino. He had just reached the legal age for the presidency and was beginning to gain much national popularity. Manila's mayor, Antonio J. Villegas, also sought the nomination with Senator Genaro Magsaysay, younger brother of the late President Magsaysay. Magsaysay, like Marcos, moved to the Liberal Party from the Nacionalista, as had Marcos, to avail himself of a nomination for presidential candidate; however, it was Senator Sergio Osmeña, Jr., from Cebu City, in the southern Philippines, and son of the late President Sergio Osmeña, Sr., who captured the presidential nomination. Magsaysay was chosen as his runningmate.

The 1969 election was marked by a lack of ideological differences between the candidates. Both hurled accusations against each other. It was a contest of popularity and also of force. There was considerable violence related to the election. Those in power, especially, resorted to fraud and to intimidating voters, and in some places ballot boxes were stolen.[93]

Marcos accused Osmeña of collaborating with the Japanese during World War II by doing business with the occupation forces. Osmeña, on the other hand, harped on Marcos's inability to fulfill his 1965 election promises. With the intent of playing on some pro-American sentiments among Filipino voters, he also accused Marcos of being anti-American. In foreign policy, Osmeña endorsed American bases and foreign investment, and was anti-Communist. Marcos, in contrast, rode a crest of growing nationalism at least in his rhetoric. Because of its involvement in Vietnam, the United States was becoming more and more unpopular with some Filipinos. Marcos sounded as if he wanted an independent foreign policy. He called for the renegotiation of U.S.-Philippine treaties "towards greater equality characterized by mutual respect and achievement." If elected in November, he said, he would continue a cautious open-door policy on trade and cultural relations with the Soviet Union, the People's Republic of China, and other socialist countries.[94] He foresaw the eventual withdrawal of the United States from the mainland of Southeast Asia and Nixon's policy of detente as well as other changes in U.S. policy on the Soviet Union and China. Marcos played the role of the nationalist and gained his desired advantage. He argued the advantage of continuity of administration and in his fiery rhetoric drowned Osmeña's bland speeches and sagging look. Marcos dominated the polls. He broke the tradition of an incumbent not running for reelection. He gathered 5,017,343 votes against Osmeña's 3,043,122.[95]

AFTERMATH OF THE ELECTION

Disaster followed the 1969 election. In order to win, Marcos "used up the government's foreign exchange reserves and left the country with few resources to cover a huge trade deficit and to service or pay interest on the mounting external debt."[96] The net deficit in the balance of payments for 1969 was 934 million pesos, more than three times larger than the deficit for the previous year and roughly equal to the cumulative deficits between 1961 and 1968.[97]

There was a dramatic increase in the money supply especially during the last four months of 1969, the campaign period. The money supply rose from 4 million pesos in August to 4.8 million pesos in December. The increase in the money supply was related to the large balance-of-payments deficit. According to Robert Baldwin, Central Bank loans to the national government together with securities of the national government held by the Central Bank rose by 445 million pesos in the last six months, and national government securities held by commercial banks increased by 219 million pesos in the same time period.[98]

Restrictive economic and fiscal policies were imposed. Import letters of credit were limited, as was open account financing of certain basic consumer and producer goods. The government limited the supply of foreign exchange for commercial banks and raised the reserve requirements of commercial, rural, savings, and development banks.[99]

By the end of 1969, the Philippines faced public and private foreign debts of $1.6 billion; $40 million of the total was due by 1970, and the rest within four years. The payment due for 1970 was divided among the Central Bank ($196 million), the government ($58 million), and the private sector ($198 million).[100] With a monetary crisis of such proportions, the desperate Philippine government asked the International Monetary Fund (IMF) and the World Bank for help. Assistance came to the Philippines on the condition that the peso be devalued more than 60% against the dollar. The strategy of the World Bank and the IMF temporarily relieved the balance-of-payments deficit, with the devaluation resulting in increasing foreign exchange; however, domestic inflation also increased.

Nineteen seventy marked not only deteriorating economic conditions but also marked growing opposition to the established government, criticism of the holders of power, and calls for societal reform. While Marcos was outside the halls of Congress delivering his State-of-the-Nation address in 1970, some 20,000 students, workers, and farmers demonstarted against him. As the Marcoses emerged from the Congress building, stones and bottles were thrown at them. They were not hurt, but about 300 students and seventy-three policemen were injured in a clash between police and demonstrators. Members of Congress and the media charged that the police were brutal and used unreasonable force. Then a series of street fights started in December 29, 1969, when a "student threw a small impotent bomb toward the car carrying Vice-President [Spiro] Agnew, who was in Manila to attend inauguration ceremonies."[101] Violence escalated further toward the end of January and culminated in the "Battle of Mendiola."

Student demonstrations, teach-ins, walkouts, and rallies persisted during the year. They shouted, "Down with fascism, imperialism, and bureaucratic capitalism." Students denounced not only the Marcos government but the United States as well, asserting that Marcos was a U.S. puppet. It was not surprising, therefore, that areas near the U.S. embassy on Roxas Boulevard were a frequent site of demonstrations. In February "rampaging youth stormed the U.S. embassy after a mass rally."[102] Demonstrations persisted until April, when the school year ended. By then, the youth had been organized into several groups and associations such as the Kabataang Makabayan (Nationalist Youth), the National Students Union, and the Movement for Democratic Philippines (MDP). Those student organizations engaged workers, teachers, and professors in open criticism of the government. To propagate social criticism, they also conducted "teach-ins" among fellow students, factory workers, farmers, and labor union members. School newspapers were also forums for discussion. Manila's plazas and parks were often sites for rallies. Student groups marched in the streets carrying placards and burning effigies. The "parliament of the streets" also became a forum for expressing frustration with rising prices, unemployment, abuses by people who had wealth and authority, the yawning gap between the rich and poor, and the lack of social opportunity.[103]

In a Philippine Senate report in 1967, Senator Manuel P. Manahan stated that if the people, particularly of Central Luzon, did not have their lot improved, they might be persuaded to join an armed rebellion with the Huks. Expressions of dissatisfaction with the social order ranged from the Lapiang Malaya (Free Party) "uprising" in 1967 to the reestablishment of the Communist Party in December 1968.

On Sunday morning of May 21, 1967, Philippine Constabulary (PC) troopers had an encounter with the religious-political organization Lapiang Malaya. The PC used automatic weapons in its confrontation with the machete-wielding members of the Lapiang. Thirty-three Lapiang members were killed, and seventeen others were wounded. The party's members were armed only with what they believed to be sacred machetes (*bolos*), amulets, and "bullet-defying" uniforms. The leader of the Lapiang was an eighty-six-year-old Bicolano named Valentin de los Santos. A charismatic leader, he was said to be in communication with the Bathala (Supreme God) and Filipino patriots like Jose Rizal. He believed that the attainment of freedom was linked with the Second Coming as prophesied in the New Testament.

Before the uprising, he demanded the resignation of Marcos, who, he believed, was favoring alien powers. The Lapian was planning to march to Malacañang Palace to receive the resignation of Marcos and oversee the surrender of arms by the armed forces, but the marchers did not reach their destination. They instead clashed with PC troopers. Their Lapian headquarters were raided and the rest of their members rounded up. De los Santos, whose stated goals were "true justice, true equality, and true freedom," was taken into custody and pronounced insane. Mauled and beaten while sleeping with the hopelessly insane cases with whom he was interned, he lost consciousness and was put in isolation. "After more than a week, he died without regaining consciousness."[104]

On March 29, 1969, the New People's Army (NPA) was born. Its nascence was based on the proposition that "political power grows out of the barrel of a gun." The pursuit of armed struggle was believed to be the means for the liberation of the oppressed. Commander Dante seceded from the Hukbong Magpapalaya ng Bayan and joined with the reestablished Communist Party of Amado Guerrero.[105] He seceded from Commander Sumulong's group, who according to Nemenzo, "feel out of PKP (Partido Komunista ng Pilipinas) control and quickly degenerated into a crime syndicate" running a protection racket outside Clark Air Base, providing protection for American military construction projects, and breaking strikes by Filipino employees inside Clark Air Base.[106]

Through 1969 and 1970, according to Philippine government sources, the New People's Army had more than sixty clashes with either the PC or the army. Those clashes involved hit-and-run attacks or sudden attacks on patrols.[107] It was not clear "who was killing whom and why."[108] It was possible that assassination squads were on the run and collusion existed among the Huks, government forces, and criminals, particularly in Central Luzon and especially around Clark Air Base and Angeles City. The upsurge of violence can be attributed to economic miseries, political bickering, and feuds. The poor increasingly resorted to crimes such as robbery and burglary. Manila newspapers fed on the growing crime and on the political battles being waged in government halls for favors and patronage.[109]

In the early 1970s, the Philippines became an acute case of imbalances in economic distribution. Statistical indicators in the *Far Eastern Economic Review* showed that those imbalances could have become volatile. The Review's *Asia Yearbook* stated that "only 2.6% of Filipino families earn[ed] 10,000 (US$1,538) or more a year; 6.8% earn[ed] 5,000 pesos to 9,999 pesos (US$769-1,538) only 13.5% earn[ed] 3,000 pesos to 4,999 pesos (US$461-769). The rest 77.1% earn[ed] far below 3,000 pesos (US$461), with 11.7% marking below 500 pesos (US$76) per annum."[110]

Dissatisfaction and social rifts were widespread all the way to the upper echelons of government. Two newly commissioned officers of the armed forces defected to the ranks of the Communist rebels. Lt. Victor Corpuz, who had recently graduated with honors from the Philippine Military Academy (PMA), defected from the corps. He led a raid on the academy's armory, seized guns and armaments, and joined the New People's Army. Lt. Crispin Tagamolila, another honor graduate, resigned from his PC appointment because of his extreme dissatisfaction and frustration with the military. The Philippine military later killed Tagamolila.

On January 14, 1971, Vice-President Fernando Lopez resigned as secretary of agriculture after Marcos excoriated him. Marcos charged that Lopez was responsible for undermining government reforms and programs. Marcos had laid the blame for the ills of Philippine society on the so-called oligarchs. That blame was an attempt to defuse radical and militant criticism to other sectors of government and society other than to Marcos himself. Marcos blamed the oligarchs who were characterized as men of power and wealth and as holders of business conglomerates. The critics could then hound them rather than Marcos. The Lopez family, which held various interests in utilities, sugar, media, and other industries, earned the ire of Marcos because of the critical reception Marcos received in the *Manila Chronicle*, a Lopez-owned daily newspaper. Marcos also had his eye on the Manila Electric Company (Meralco), dominated by the Lopez family, and it was rumored that he envied the family's wealth. The president ordered a probe of Meralco and other Lopez holdings. Later, after martial law was imposed in 1972, he would take over the enterprise.

The Laurels from Batangas, another political and wealthy family, broke off with the Marcoses; then Congressman Jose B. Laurel was ousted from the speakership of the House of Representatives. Rafael Salas, Marcos's executive secretary—a position popularly known as "Little President"—resigned from the cabinet. He spoke of a "long period of disenchantment" and that "he felt he was just being used as a 'shield' for those [of our] colleagues, who were intent only on monkey business and raking [in] money."[111] In his administration, Salas was noted for his management of the tree-planting program and for Masagana 99, the campaign to increase rice production. Marcos claimed the success of the campaign as his own. In spite of his able performance, Salas had not been considered by Marcos for the senatorial lineup.[112]

Senator Jose Diokno, a leading member of the ruling Nacionalista Party, but a vocal and independent critic of the Marcos administration, resigned from the party after the bombing at Plaza Miranda in August 1971.

Plaza Miranda was a symbol of free expression in the Philippines. President Magsaysay's famously quoted response to anyone proposing a law was "Can we defend this at Plaza Miranda?" It is a square bounded by the busy downtown stores in the Quiapo district and the Quiapo church, the Shrine of Jesus Christ, the Black Nazarene. It was a frequent site of rallies and demonstrations of both established parties as well as of radical groups and government critics. Many public transportation lines, both jeepneys and buses, converge on the Plaza Miranda, and it is a center for shoppers, pedestrians, hawkers, and even underworld characters.

On the night of August 21, 1971, the Liberal Party was staging a rally for the midterm election. The rally included the eight candidates for the senatorial slate. Two fragmentation grenades were thrown onto the platform, killing eleven persons and injuring around ninety. Liberal Party leaders Senators Sergio Osmeña, Jr., Gerardo Roxas, and Jovito Salonga and Manila mayoralty candidate Ramon D. Bagatsing were among those severely injured, the latter partly disabled. Marcos denounced the bombing as a heinous crime and suspended the writ of habeas corpus. He ordered the arrest of leaders of nationalist groups, including four members of the Kabataang Makabayan (Nationalist Youth) and Dr. Nemesio Prudente, president of the Philippine College of Commerce. Later, more than 100 were arrested in an alleged terrorist-Communist plot to bomb several strategic places in Manila.

Thousands marched in the streets to protest the Plaza Miranda bombing and to oppose the suspension of habeas corpus. Diokno, upon his resignation from the ruling party, charged that "military men trained by the military threw grenades, not Communists as charged by Marcos," and that "fragments of grenades found at the plaza indicate that it came from an army armory."[113]

Marcos charged that Senator Aquino was part of the conspiracy and that he aided the Communist subversives by giving them weapons, ammunitions, and other support. Marcos further charged that Aquino was a Communist himself. The president warned that he would do everything to prevent Aquino from becoming president, even if it meant letting Mrs. Marcos vie for the presidency.[114]

The legality of suspending habeas corpus was questioned in the Supreme Court, but the Supreme Court upheld the president's actions in the case of *Lansang v. Garcia*.

In his testimony before the U.S. Congress, Primitivo Mijares stated that the Philippine Supreme Court was not spared from Marcos's manipulation. He declared that "when Marcos took over the presidency he figured that in a span of six years, nine of the eleven seats in the Supreme Court would become vacant, hence he could pack the tribunal with his own men . . . [and] by the time martial law was proclaimed . . . only three justices were non-Marcos appointees."[115]

It was clear to a number of observers that Marcos was consolidating power in order to establish a dictatorship. Many already feared that he would not hesitate to impose martial law so that he could rule indefinitely. In a television interview reported by the *New York Times*, Marcos stated that he would impose martial law should there be a threat coming from Communist terrorists that would lead to the collapse of the civilian government.[116] A few months before that interview, it was also reported that he was weighing the possibility of imposing martial law. A fortune teller predicted that he would be "threatened with assassination before April," and he wanted to strengthen his position.[117] Attempts to influence the deliberations and outcome of the Constitutional Convention were another indication of Marcos's intent to continue his presidency beyond 1973.

The January 23, 1971, issue of the Philippines' *Free Press* magazine described a method for imposing martial law. It would be imposed more than a year later. The method was described thusly:

With the Courts and Congress reduced to impotence and the press shut up—with publishers who dare to disagree with Marcos placed under house arrest or in concentration camps where they would be joined sooner or later by outraged justices of the Supreme Court, senators and representatives who would not lick the boots of Marcos, as well as others who would not submit to his tyranny—the nation would be polarized. The Philippines would be divided into Marcos collaborators and those who love liberty and are branded as misguided elements and declared enemies of the Marcos state.[118]

In July 1972, Senator Diokno proposed in a speech that even if Marcos could impose martial law, he could not legally be president after December 30, 1973, the date his constitutional term was supposed to end. Diokno asserted that "only naked force" could enable Marcos to remain in office. Diokno cited Article VII, Section 4, of the Philippine Constitution, which states that the president's term of office "shall end at noon on the thirtieth day of December, four years after his election, and the term of his successor would begin from such time." Section 5 further states "No person shall serve as president for more than eight consecutive years," nor can that person interrupt those eight years by "voluntary renunciation of the office for any length of time." Diokno concluded that even if martial law were declared, Marcos should vacate the presidency, turn it over to Senate President Gil Puyat, as his constitutional successor, until a new president is elected and sworn in. Diokno's speech, entitled "Throne of Bayonets," was in some ways prophetic. Marcos did declare martial rule and used naked force to remain in office. Marcos, however, was adroit enough to supply legal and constitutional justification for his continuance in office.

Marcos's idea for declaring martial law and his messianic visions of reforming society were also hinted at in his book *Today's Revolution Democracy*. In the book, he mentioned a "new society," a term he later used to describe the era of martial law.[119]

In the Senate, using information leaked to him by friends of friends in the military, Aquino revealed the existence of "Oplan Sagittarius." "Oplan Sagittarius" outlined the imposition of martial law. According to Reuben R. Canoy in his book *Counterfeit Revolution*, a military informant told Aquino that Oplan Sagittarius was the master plan of a multi-faceted operation for the declaration of martial law: the apparatus, the scheme, the mechanism of martial law itself. Sagittarius also provided the legal basis for Proclamation 1081, by enumerating the conditions and situations that made martial law necessary. "It contained a detailed account of the places targeted for military take-over (such as airports, shipping ports, communication networks, transportation networks, the mass media, the guns and ammunition, the loose firearms of the citizenry . . .) [and it] also named special units that were to implement the initial takeover, with the backing of the entire armed forces in the Philippines, if ever the need arose."[120]

It was alleged that a plan of action had existed as early as 1965. Even with Aquino's revelation, no one opposed the plan because no one was certain that the plan would be carried out. As for identifying the person who leaked the plan, Mijares gave a hint. He said that when the plan for imposing martial law was finalized, he distributed copies to various high-ranking officials in the military and the intelligence network. The names of the recipients of the distributed copies were zodiac signs corresponding to the first letter or initial of the surname of the person who received the plan. The copy coded "Sagittarius" went to General Marcos Soliman; thus, when the plan was made public, other military men who had knowledge of some plan did not know of the existence of "Oplan Sagittarius." They knew of a plan with a different zodiac name.[121] Marcos had carefully planned the project so that if someone turned on him, he would be able to take immediate action.

Marcos conferred with the military many times before he put into action a plan that would succeed only with their support. The military, after gaining strength and capability under the aegis of Marcos, became the foundation and support of the making of authoritarian government.

NOTES

1. William Manchester, *The American Caesar: Douglas MacArthur 1880-1964* (New York: Dell, 1978), pp. 47-48.

2. Frederica Bunge, ed., *Philippines: A Country Study* (Washington, DC: Foreign Area Studies, American University, 1983), p. 61.

3. William Henry Scott, "The Creation of a Cultural Minority," in *Cracks in the Parchment Curtain and Other Essays in Philippine History* (Quezon City: New Day Publishers, 1982), pp. 28-41.

4. Anti-Slavery Society, *The Philippines: Authoritarian Government, Multinationals and Ancestral Lands*, Indigenous People's Development Series No. 1, 1983 (London: Anti-Slavery Society, 1983), p. 15.

5. Walden Bello, David Kinley, and Elaine Elinson, *Development Debacle: The World Bank in the Philippines* (San Francisco: Institute for Food and Development Policy — Philippine Solidarity Network, 1982), pp. 101-103.

6. Ibid.

7. Ibid.

8. CHRP, *Fact Sheet on the Philippines*, p. 1.

9. John Leddy Phelan, *The Hispanization of the Philippines: Spanish Aims and Filipino Responses, 1565-1700* (Madison: University of Wisconsin Press, 1959).

10. Peter Gowing and Robert D. McAmis, eds., *Muslim Filipinos: Their History, Society, and Contemporary Problems* (Manila: Solidaridad, 1974); and Cesar Adib Majul, *Muslims in the Philippines* (Quezon City: University of the Philippines Press, 1973).

11. Anti-Slavery Society, *Philippines*, Chapters 3 and 7.

12. Majul, *Muslims*; and for an excellent background of Mindanao history during the Spanish period, see Horacio de la Costa, *The Jesuits in the Philippines, 1581-1768* (Cambridge, MA: Harvard University Press, 1967).

13. David Joel Steinberg, *The Philippines: A Singular and a Plural Place* (Boulder, CO: Westview Press, 1982), p. ix.

14. The United States granted the Philippines its political independence on July 4, 1946. July 4 is now celebrated as Filipino-American Friendship Day.

15. Fred Eggan, "Philippine Social Structure," in George M. Guthrie, *Six Perspectives on the Philippines* (Manila: Bookmark, 15.1971), p. 4.

16. See Note 1.

17. For a description of pre-Hispanic culture of the Philippines and Philippine culture society at the Spanish contact, the following firsthand accounts are helpful: Antonio de Morga, *Sucesos de las Islas Filipinas*(1604) *as Filipinas*; Pedro Chirino, *Relacion de las Islas*; Juan de Plasencia, *Relacion de las costumbres . . .* ; and Miguel de Loarca, *Relacion de las Islas Filipinas* (1582). These accounts are translated in Emma Helen Blair and James Alexander Robertson, *The Philippine Islands, 1493-1803*, 55 vol. (Cleveland: Arthur Clark Co., 1903).

18. Nicholas P. Cushner, *Spain in the Philippines from Conquest to Revolution* (Quezon City: Ateneo de Manila University Press, Institute of Philippine Culture, 1971), pp. 9-10; and Blair and Robertson, "Papal Bull of Alexander VI," *Philippine Islands,* Vol. 1.

19. Phelan, *Hispanization*, pp. 70-71.

20. Cushner, *Spain in the Philippines*, pp. 155-168.

21. From Onofre D. Corpuz, *Bureaucracy in the Philippines* (Manila: University of the Philippines Institute of Public Administration), pp. 46-47.

22. Renato Constantino, *The Philippines: A Past Revisited* (Quezon City: Tala Publishing Services, 1975), pp. 58-59.

23. Bonifacio S. Salamanca, "Background and Early Beginnings of the Encomienda in the Philippines," *Philippine Social Sciences and Humanities Review* (March 1961): 69-71.

24. Corpuz, *Bureaucracy*, p. 94.

25. De la Costa, *Jesuits*, pp. 642-643.

26. William Lytle Schurz, *The Manila Galleon* (New York: Dutton, 1959).

27. Corpuz, *Bureaucracy*, p. 102.

28. Horacio de la Costa, *Readings in Philippine History: Selected Texts Presented with Commentary* (Manila: Bookmark, 1965), pp. 115-118.

29. Leslie E. Bauzon, "Philippine Agrarian Reform, 1880-1965: The Revolution That Never Was" (paper read at the University of the Philippines, School of Economics, March 7, 1975).

30. Vicente B. Valdepenas, Jr., and Gemelino M. Bautista, *The Emergence of the Philippine Economy* (Manila: Papyrus Press, 1977), pp. 86-109.

31. Hundreds of revolts were staged against Spanish rule. See Constantino, *Philippines: A Past Revisited*; and David Sturtevant, *Popular Uprisings in the Philippines, 1840-1940* (Ithaca, NY: Cornell University Press, 1976).

32. Edgar Wickberg, "The Chinese Mestizo in Philippine History," *Journal of Southeast Asian History* (March 1964): 62-100; and Edgar Wickberg, *The Chinese in Philippine Life, 1850-1898* (New Haven, CT: Yale University Press, 1965).

33. John H. Schumacher, *The Propaganda Movement, 1880-1895* (Manila: Solidaridad Publishing House, 1973).

34. Jose Rizal, *Noli Me Tangere* and *El Filibusterismo*; Leon Ma Guerrero, *The First Filipino: A Biography of Jose Rizal* (Manila: National Historical Institute, 1977).

35. Teodoro A. Agoncillo, *The Revolt of the Masses: The Story of Bonifacio and the Katipunan* (Quezon City: University of the Philippines, 1956).

36. Eliodoro Robles, *The Philippines in the Nineteenth Century* (Quezon City: Malaya Books, 1969), p. 184.

37. Alejandro M. Fernandez, *The Philippines and the United States: The Forging of New Relations* (Quezon City: NSDB-UP Integrated Research Program, 1977), pp. 33-34.

38. Teodoro A. Agoncillo, *Malolos: The Crisis of the Republic* (Quezon City: University of the Philippines, 1960), pp. 187-188, 213-214.

39. Alejandro M. Fernandez, *International Law in Philippine Relations, 1898-1946* (Quezon City: University of the Philippines Press, 1971); Leandro H. Fernandez, *The Philippine Republic* (New York: AMS Press, 1926; Reprinted 1968); Teodoro M. Kalaw, *The Philippine Revolution* (Manila: Manila Book Co., 1925).

40. Stuart Creighton Miller, *"Benevolent Assimilation": The American Conquest of the Philippines, 1899-1903* (New Haven, CT: Yale University Press, 1982).

41. Garel A. Grunder and William E. Livezey, *The Philippines and the United States* (Norman: University of Oklahoma Press, 1951), p. 51.

42. John R. M. Taylor, *Philippine Insurrection against the United States*, edited by Renato Constantino (Pasay City: Eugenio Lopez Foundation, 1971), is a collection of documents on the war.

43. Romeo V. Cruz, "The Filipino Collaboration with the Americans, 1899-1902," *Comment* 10 (1st Qrtr. 1960): 10-29; Onofre D. Corpuz, *The Philippines* (Englewood Cliffs, NJ: Prentice Hall, Inc., 1965), p. 65, used the term "cooptation."

44. Teodoro A. Agoncillo and Oscar M. Alfonso, *A Short History of the Filipino People* (Manila: University of the Philippines, 1960), discusses the period of suppressed nationalism.

45. Bonifacio S. Salamanca, *The Filipino Reaction to American Rule, 1901-1913* (Hamden, CT: Shoestring Press, 1968); Theodore Friend, *Between Two Empires: The Ordeal of the Philippines* (New Haven, CT: Yale University Press, 1965); and Norman G. Owen, *Compadre Colonialism: Studies on the Philippines under American Rule*, Michigan Papers on South and Southeast Asia No. 3 (Ann Arbor: University of Michigan Press, 1971).

46. Peter W. Stanley, *A Nation in the Making: The Philippines and the United States, 1899-1921* (Cambridge, MA: Harvard University Press, 1974), pp. 204ff.

47. Robert Pringle, *Indonesia and the Philippines: American Interests in Island Southeast Asia* (New York: Columbia University Press, 1980), pp. 54-55.

48. Salamanca, *Filipino Reaction*, pp. 55-56.

49. Ibid., p. 58, quoted from James LeRoy.

50. Corpuz, *Philippines*, p. 99.

51. James C. Thompson, Jr., Peter W. Stanley, and John Curtis Perry, *Sentimetal Imperialists: The American Experiences in East Asia* (New York: Harper and Row, 1981), p. 119.

52. Benito Legarda and Roberto Y. Garcia, "Economic Collaboration: The Trading Relationship," in Frank H. Golay, ed., *Philippine-American Relations* (Manila: Solidaridad Publishing House, 1966), pp. 125-148; Laura J. Henze, "U.S.-Philippine Economic Relations and Trade Negotiations," *Asian Survey* 16:4 (April 1976): 319-337.

53. For the basic literature on the Japanese occupation of the Philippines, see Teodoro A. Agoncillo, *The Fateful Years: Japan's Adventure in the Philippines,* 2 vols. (Quezon City: R. P. Garcia Publishing, 1965); and David Joel Steinberg, *Philippine Collaboration in World War II* (Ann Arbor: University of Michigan Press, 1967).

54. Steinberg, *Philippines: A Singular and a Plural Place*, pp. 53-54.

55. Jovito R. Salonga, "The Marcos Dictatorship and a Vision of Government" (unpublished manuscript). Los Angeles, 1984, p. 343.

56. The Second Ordinance appended to the Philippine Constitution is the parity amendment whereas the Laurel-Langley [Trade] Agreement is the "Agreement . . . Between the Republic of the Philippines and the U.S. Concerning Trade and Related Matters during a Transitional Period Following the Institution of Philippine Independence; Signed at Washington, D.C., September 6, 1955." Appendices 9 and 22 respectively of Alejandro M. Fernandez, *The Philippines and the U.S.*

57. S. R. Shalom, *The United States and the Philippines: A Study of Neocolonialism* (Philadelphia: Institute for the Study of Human Issues, 1981), pp. 38ff.

58. Fernandez, *The Philippines and the U.S.*, Appendices 12 and 18, for the Military Bases Agreement and the Mutual Defense Treaty.

59. Emmanuel Pelaez, "Philippine Foreign Policy: The Whole and Its Parts," in Jose V. Abueva and Raul P. de Guzman, eds., *Foundations and Dynamics of Filipino Government and Politics* (Manila: Bookmark, 1969), pp. 487ff.

60. For first hand accounts and discussions of CIA activities in the Philippines, see Edward Lansdale, *In the Midst of Wars: An American's Mission to South East Asia* (New York: Harper and Row, 1972); Joseph Burkholder Smith, *Portrait of a Cold Warrior: Second Thoughts of a Top CIA Agent* (New York: Ballantine Books, 1976); Jose V. Abueva, *Ramon Magsaysay: A Political Biography* (Manila Solidaridad Publishing House, 1971); and Shalom, *The United States*, Chapters 3 and 4; for a history and analysis of the Huk rebellion, see Benedict Kerkvliet, *The Huk Rebellion: A Study of Peasant Revolt in the Philippines* (Berkeley: University of California Press, 1977).

61. Corpuz, *The Philippines*, p. 95.

62. David Rosenberg, "The End of the Freest Press in the World," *Bulletin of Concerned Asian Scholars* 5:1 (July 1973).

63. Frank Lynch, "Social Acceptance Reconsidered," in Frank Lynch and Alfonso de Guzman II, eds., *Four Readings on Philippine Values*, 4th ed. (Quezon City: Ateneo de Manila University Press, 1973), p. 15.

64. Carl H. Lande, "Party Politics in the Philippines," in George M. Guthrie, ed., *Six Perspectives on the Philippines* (Manila: Bookmark, 1971).

65. Ibid., p. 95.

66. John Duncan Power, "Peasant Society and Clientelist Politics," *American Political Science Review* 64 (June 1970): 412.

67. Mary Racelis Hollnsteiner, *The Dynamics of Power in a Philippine Municipality* (Quezon City: Community Development Research Council, University of the Philippines, 1963), p.129.

68. Corpuz, *The Philippines*, p. 99.

69. See Hollnsteiner, *Dynamics*, Chapter 5, for a description of Filipino behavior in elections.

70. Ibid., lider comes from the English word "leader." Usually the most influential person in the village, a *lider* is approached by political parties and candidates to reach the electors and constituents.

71. Ibid., p. 109.

72. Ibid.

73. Bauzon, "Philippine Agrarian Reform."

74. Remigio E. Agpalo, *Pandango sa Ilaw: The Politics of Oriental Mindoro* (Ohio: Ohio University Center for International Studies, 1969), p. 4, quoted in Reynaldo Clemena Ileto, *Pasyon and Revolution: Popular Movements in the Philippines, 1840-1910* (Quezon City: Ateneo de Manila University Press,1979).Politicians are popularly perceived as corrupt and depraved. A classical portrayal of a politician can be gleaned from a Tagalog novel by Celso Al. Carunungan, *Satanas sa Lupa (Satan on Earth)*.

75. Ileto, *Pasyon*, p. 13.

76. Dapen Liang, *Philippine Parties and Politics: A Historical Study of National Experience in Democracy* (San Francisco: Gladstone Co., 1970), pp. 281ff.

77. Ibid., pp. 343ff.

78. For a standard biography of Marcos written for his presidential campaigns, see Hartzell Spence, *Marcos of the Philippines: A Biography* (New York: World Publishing Co., 1969), issued in 1964 as *For Every Tear a Victory*.

79. Marcos was showing off his twenty-seven war medals to reporters when one journalist pointed to a replica of the U.S. Congressional Medal of Honor. Marcos was angered and laid blame for this mistake on his overzealous assistants. *Newsweek*, January 24, 1983, p. 43.

80. The authorized biography of Imelda Marcos was written by Kerima Polotan-Tuvera, wife of Marcos' assistant. A controversial biography banned from circulation, *The Untold Story of Imelda Marcos*, was written by Carmen Navarro Pedrosa.

81. See Robert Shaplen, *A Turning Wheel: Three Decades of Asian Report; Revolution as Witnessed by a Correspondent for the New Yorker* (New York: Random House, 1979), pp. 214ff, for a description of Marcos's personality.

82. Claude A. Buss, *The United States and the Philippines: Background for Policy* (Washington, DC: American Enterprise Institute for Public Policy Research; and Stanford: Hoover Institute on War, Revolution and Peace, 1977), p. 46.

83. Art. VI, Sec. 2-4, the 1935 Philippines Constitution, in Gregorio F. Zaide, *Philippine Government: Development, Organization, and Function* (Manila: Modern Book Company, 1965), 280-281.

84. Jean Grossholtz, "The Philippines: New Adventure with Old Problems," *Asian Survey* 9:1 (January 1969): 54.

85. Benigno S. Aquino, Jr., "What's Wrong with the Philippines?" *Foreign Affairs* 46:4 (July 1968): 770-779.

86. Grossholtz, "Philippines," pp. 52-53.

87. Ibid., p. 53.

88. Amado Guerrero, *Philippine Society and Revolution* (Hong Kong: Tang Ku Pao, 1971), p. 197.

89. Jose V. Abueva, "The Philippines: Tradition and Change," *Asian Survey* (January 1970): 63.

90. Robert O. Tilman, "The Philippines in 1970: A Difficult Decade Begins," *Asian Survey* (January 1971): 140.

91. Abueva, "The Philippines," p. 62.

92. Grossholtz, "Philippines," p. 56.

93. Violence and bribery decided the results of the 1969 elections. Ramon Diaz, former member of the Presidential Commission on Good Government, recounted stories about this in an interview with the author in Los Angeles, 1985.

94. *New York Times*, October 27, 1969, p. 18.

95. Abueva, "The Philippines," p. 56.

96. Bello, Kinley, and Elinson, *Development Debacle*, p. 21.

97. Robert E. Baldwin, *The Philippines: Foreign Trade Regimes and Economic Development* (New York: National Bureau of Economic Research, 1975), p. 73.

98. Ibid.

99. Ibid., pp. 76-77.

100. Ibid.

101. Tilman, "Philippines in 1970," p. 141.

102. *New York Times*, February 19, 1970, p. 3.

103. Crispin Aranda, "1st Quarter Storm," *Philippine News*, February 1-7, 1984, p. 13.

104. Sturtevant, *Popular Uprisings*, p. 22; *New York Times*, May 21, 1967, p. 5; Ileto, *Pasyon*, pp. 1-3.

105. Francisco Nemenzo, "Rectification Process in the Philippine Communist Movement," (revised version of a paper prepared for the seminar workshop on "Armed Communism in Southeast Asia," Institute of Southeast Asian Studies, Singapore, 1979), p. 11.

106. Ibid.

107. Justus M. van der Kroef, "Communism and Reform in the Philippines," *Pacific Affairs*, 46:1 (spring 1973): 37.

108. Grossholtz, "Philippines," p. 54-55.

109. Harvey A. Averch et al., *The Matrix of Policy in the Philippines* (Princeton, NJ: Princeton University Press, 1971), p. 115ff.

110. Far Eastern Economic Review, *Asia Yearbook 1973*, p. 253.

111. Ibid.

112. Salas then assumed a position in the international civil service as executive director of the United Nations Fund on Population based in New York.

113. *New York Times*, September 7, 1971, p. 11.

114. Ibid., September 14, 1971, p. 10.

115. Primitivo Mijares, *The Conjugal Dictatorship of Ferdinand and Imelda Marcos I* (San Francisco: Union Square Publications, 1976), p. 134.

116. *New York Times*, April 5, 1970, p. 4.

117. Ibid., February 21, 1970, p. 3. Marcos was superstitious in regards to the use of numbers and dates. Important proclamations, referendums, or elections were held, dated, or numbered with numbers 7, 11, or 21.

118. *Free Press*, January 23, 1971.

119. Ferdinand E. Marcos, *The Democratic Revolution in the Philippines*, Chapter 4, pp. 105ff.

120. Reuben R. Canoy, *The Counterfeit Revolution: Martial Law in the Philippines* (Manila: Philippine Editions Publishing, 1980), pp. 17-18.

121. Mijares, *Conjugal Dictatorship*, p. 143. General Soliman was reported to have died of a heart attack after martial law was imposed.

Chapter 3

Martial Law and Regime Legitimation

The accumulation of all powers, legislative, executive, and judiciary, in the same hands . . . may justly be pronounced the very definition of tyranny.[1]

MARTIAL LAW

In spite of the warnings and imminent signs that martial law might be imposed, Filipinos were caught by surprise on the morning of September 23, 1972. It was a Saturday, but one different from all previous Saturdays. None of the radio or television stations was functioning. Filipinos who were used to listening to morning talk and news programs, as well as commentaries from their favorite radio announcers, wondered if something was wrong. The early morning broadcast was prime time in the Philippines, and Filipinos were used to getting their news early. Filipinos who got their news from the newspaper, that morning waited quite a long time. In the streets of Manila, there was fear and wonder about what was going on.

As the day passed, word spread that martial law had been imposed. That evening when radio and television stations came back to life again, the voice of the president's press secretary, Francisco Tatad, sounded on the air. He read Proclamation 1081, which placed the entire Philippines under martial law. Pausing only for a few seconds to gulp water, he read strings of presidential decrees, general orders, and letters of instruction that implemented martial rule and paved the way for Marcos's takeover of the entire Philippine civilian and military bureaucracy. It was emphasized again and again that what was happening was not a military takeover and that civilian authority remained supreme. There were no tanks in the streets, but soldiers became prominent.

In the evening before the news blackout, the military swiftly put into effect "Oplan Sagittarius." On September 17, the president met with the group he called the "Twelve Disciples," which consisted of Secretary of Defense Juan Ponce Enrile, Armed Forces Chief of Staff Romeo C. Espino, General Rafael Zagala, Philippine Army commanding officer, General Fidel V. Ramos, PC chief, General Jose Rancudo, Philippine Air Force chief, Admiral Hilario Ruiz, Philippine Navy commander, General Fabian Ver, presidential security command chief, General

Ignacio Paz, AFP chief of intelligence, General Tomas Diaz, First PC Zone commander, General Alfredo Montoya, PC Metropolitan Command, Colonel Romeo Gatan, Rizal PC commander, and Congressman Eduardo Cojuangco, who was recalled to active duty with the rank of colonel. The president consulted with his twelve disciples about using his emergency powers.[2]

There was no indication of any threats to national security during the Philippine National Security Council meeting on September 19. The National Security Council briefing on the state of internal security gauged conditions to be between "normal" and "Internal Defense Condition No. 1," whereas the worst, or most unstable, condition was "Internal Defense Condition No. 3."[3]

On Friday evening, September 22, congressmen, senators, professors, journalists, radicals, and other potential opponents to martial law were arrested. Other potential detainees, such as Senators Raul Manglapuz and Sergio Osmena, escaped arrest because they were away from the Philippines. To prevent more opponents from escaping, the government grounded domestic air flights. Except those on special government mission, Filipinos were prohibited from traveling outside the country. The entire country was sealed off from the outside world. Overseas phone operators refused incoming phone calls. An information blackout was implemented. Various newspapers and radio and television stations were shut down by the military. The only significant dissent was a brief altercation between the military and the personnel of Eagle Broadcasting Station, a radio station housed and operated by the religious group Iglesia ni Kristo (Church of Christ). There was an exchange of fire between Iglesia ni Kristo guards in the bishop's palace grounds in Diliman and the Metropolitan Command.[4]

Police forces ordered broadcast and print media workers to leave their offices. They sealed their offices and put up signs that read: THIS BUILDING IS CLOSED AND SEALED AND PLACED UNDER MILITARY CONTROL.[5] All other forms of communication were also controlled: mimeographing machines, citizens' band radios, and shortwave radios. All school newspapers, magazines, and national publications were suspended from operation until clearance was given by martial-law authorities. In Manila, seven major English dailies, three Filipino dailies, one English-Filipino daily, eleven English weekly magazines, one Spanish daily, four Chinese dailies, three business publications, one news service, and seven television stations—and in the provinces sixty-six community newspapers and 292 radio stations—were closed.[6]

The vast network of communication was vital to the life of the Philippines. Filipinos depended on both radio and newspapers for information and communication. There was a great demand for printed matter, especially in the urban Philippines. Among Asian countries other than Japan, the Philippines has a comparatively high literacy rate. The printed media, such as newspapers, and entertainment magazines, such as comics, are staples for many people. Radio reached the remoter areas and thus was more important in the rural Philippines. Control of communication and information sources was thus necessary for any effective rule and control of the archipelago.

Marcos's first Letter of Instruction ordered Press Secretary Francisco Tatad and Defense Secretary Enrile to take control of the media. The Letter of Instruction stated:

In view of the present national emergency which has been brought about by the activities of those who are actively engaged in criminal conspiracy to seize political and state power in the Philippines and to take over the government by force and violence the extent of which has now assumed the proportion of an actual war against our people and their legitimate government, and pursuant to Proclamation 1081, dated September 21, 1972, and in my capacity as commander-in-chief of all the Armed Forces of the Philippines, and in order to prevent the use of privately-owned newspapers, magazines, radio and television facilities and all other media of communications, for propaganda purposes against the government and its duly constituted authorities or confidence of the people in our government and aggravate forewith to take over and control of all such newspapers, magazines, radio and television facilities are, for the duration of the present national emergency, you are hereby ordered forewith to take over and control all of such . . . facilities . . . wherever they are, for the duration of the present national emergency, or until otherwise ordered by me or by my duly designated representative.[7]

In the absence of unbiased sources, the people had to resort to other means of gathering information. Without the benefit of uncensored communication and nongovernment sources, people relied on word of mouth and read between the lines of official government news; however, the government threatened even those means of gathering information. Presidential Decree No. 90 made "rumor mongering" a punishable crime. Rumor mongering actually denoted any statements tantamount to criticizing the government. A former press secretary of a late president, Baldomero T. Olivera, was arrested for rumor mongering.[8]

All forms of arms were confiscated by the military, resulting in the disbanding of private armies and guards of influential politicians as well as groups called "goons." Curfew was imposed from midnight until four in the morning.

Classes at all levels from elementary school to college were suspended for a week in order to prevent any protests among students and academicians as well as to give time for the military to round up suspected subversives and dissenters. Schools did not reopen until October 14, at which time strict measures were imposed by the administration. Security guards and police officers were posted at the entrances to school buildings and grounds. Books, bags, and all student belongings brought to school were subjected to inspection. Identification cards were issued and were required to be displayed or pinned on students' uniforms at all times.

Campus politics in the Philippines was one of the most vital means of political socialization. At all levels, each class elected a set of officers to help the teacher and school administration in organizing curricular and extracurricular activities. There were also a number of organizations in schools, some social, some political, and some religious. There were also student publications and newspapers. All student publications were ordered to be registered with the Ministry of Public Information. The University of the Philippines student-operated radio station was closed by the military. The Marcos government announced that it would bring about changes in the administration and operation of schools "to protect the public interest so that university students could be protected from infiltration by radicals."[9] Despite the government's crackdown, protests and criticism persisted in schools. Throughout the martial law years, the universities never ceased to be the source of dissent and challenge to the legitimacy of authoritarianism.

At the Philippine embassy in Washington, D.C., Executive Secretary Alejandro Melchor of the Marcos cabinet, together with the Philippine ambassador to the United States, Eduardo Z. Romualdez, gave a press conference about the imposition of martial law.[10] Melchor predicted that martial law would last for two years.[11] He said it was necessary to eradicate subversion and to institute social reforms. Before reporters, Melchor and Romualdez justified the necessity of Marcos's actions. Melchor said that he expected the number of newspapers to be reduced because there were "too many" and that big business had access to the press. He alluded to the opposition-owned newspapers of what Marcos called "oligarch" families who were not in his camp.[12]

Martial law in the Philippines was newsworthy to the American media, but it did not cause concern in the government. The United States had a "special" relationship with the Philippines: the two military bases in the Philippines constituted the biggest U.S. presence outside its own territory. There were also about 800 American companies doing business in the Philippines with a total investment of around $2 billion. Indeed, the former U.S. colony had been the so-called "show case of American democracy in Asia." Historical and cultural ties bound the two countries. Many Americans served in the Philippines as teachers, soldiers, and missionaries. At the same time, a growing number of Filipinos were immigrating to the United States, especially during the 1960s when there was an upsurge of Filipino professionals such as nurses, doctors, and accountants; thus, American interest in the archipelago was maintained.

News emanating from the Philippines came with the note: "Dispatches from the Philippines were subject to official censorship." Several columns of news were devoted to changes in the Philippines in major American papers. The official U.S. government response was curt or "no comment." A State Department spokesperson, Charles W. Bray III said, "The United States was neither consulted nor did it have any advance knowledge of what Mr. Marcos planned."[13] He also said, "There was no apparent danger to United States citizens or business interests as of now." Philippine-American relations were described as excellent, so no interference was foreseen.

Meanwhile, some Filipino legislators were in Japan when martial law was imposed. House Speaker Cornelio Villareal, House Majority Floor Leader Marcelino Veloso, Nicanor Yniquez, Chairman of the House Committee on Foreign Affairs, and Senior Minority Leader Carmelo Z. Barbero of the Committee on Foreign Affairs were on a goodwill mission to Japan, the United States, Great Britain, France, and the Soviet Union. In spite of the fact that he was from the opposition party, Villareal spoke in favor of martial law, which he knew had been studied for a long time. He stated that martial law was already in effect on September 21, before it was fully imposed the following day.[14] Both he and Veloso also agreed that it was necessary to limit press freedom. They perceived, much as did Marcos, that "the enemies of the republic ride on the free press," so it was imperative to curb "the excesses of [that] freedom."[15]

Two trains of thought can be perceived from the views of Melchor in Washington and the congressmen in Japan: that the press had been perceived as the "enemy of government and its administrators" and that "big business," in opposition to the government, supported and co-conspired, as Marcos charged, with subversives. In reality, however, those "subversives" threatened Marcos's personal influence, power, and authority and marked the beginning of what David Rosenberg called a "mobilized" or "nationalized" media. Marcos took significant measures as part of the imposition of martial law, which rendered "the freest press in the world" an "institution dedicated, not to freedom of expression, but to the service of national policy and the preservation of political power."[16]

Villareal hoped that martial law would last for only five to six months, and he was not certain whether presidential elections would be held the following year.[17] The congressman's remarks reflected an uncertain attitude, shared by many, toward martial law and the absolute measures Marcos had imposed. Villareal said that martial law was not an implicit admission of the Marcos administration's inability to govern in the past seven years, but he agreed that "Mr. Marcos had not done all he might have to bring about order and reforms."[18] Congressman Barbero of the opposition expressed the ambivalent feelings of the public by saying, "as a Filipino, I wish him well, but if Mr. Marcos fails, then I regret to think of what will happen next. Any failure on his part will mean a very, very miserable future for my country."[19]

REGIME LEGITIMACY

To reduce the political cost of imposing martial law, it was important for Marcos, personally and politically, to provide a legal justification for his increasing accumulation of power; for example, six years after imposition of martial law, the term "martial law" was replaced by the terms "constitutional authoritarianism" and "crisis government." According to Benjamin Muego:

While these new labels may be dismissed by skeptical observers as transparent attempts on the part of martial law authorities to deodorize or mask the true nature of martial rule, they represent President Prime Minister Marcos's obsession with regime legitimation. The appearance of legitimacy, or the primacy of the rule of law and adherence to "constitutional processes," is necessary not only to ensure the continued acquiescence of the majority of Filipinos but also to placate the U.S., whose support the Marcos regime needs in order to survive.[20]

Even before he imposed martial law, Marcos attempted to perpetuate his power by calling a constitutional convention to adopt a new constitution that would allow him more than two terms in office, a provision not included in the 1935 Constitution. His attempt failed, so Marcos imposed martial law to ensure the ratification of the new constitution.

CONSTITUTIONAL CONVENTION OF 1971

The public believed that the old constitution needed to be changed when Marcos called for a convention to ratify a new constitution. It was believed that the form of government and other state practices should be updated to respond more effectively to current Philippine needs. Some quarters asserted that the Philippine constitution was a colonial document. It was formulated to establish the Philippine Commonwealth as mandated by the Tydings-McDuffie Law, a U.S. congressional act providing for a transition period as a preparation for Philippine independence on July 4, 1946. The 1935 Constitution, as it is also known, was formulated by a constitutional convention whose delegates were elected by Philippine citizens, approved in a plebiscite by the Filipinos, and signed by an American president, Franklin Delano Roosevelt.

The 1935 Constitution shared many characteristics with the U.S. Constitution. It provided for a government with three principal branches. The executive was placed under the president, popularly elected every four years. Legislative power was vested in a bicameral legislature, the Congress. The Senate was the upper house with twenty-four members elected at large. The House of Representatives was elected by geographical districts. It consisted of more than 100 representatives from various provinces of the Philippines. The power of the judicial branch of government was vested in an eleven-member Supreme Court. Inferior or lower courts were to be creations of law. Independent constitutional officers such as the Commission on Elections and the General Auditing Office were also created.

Three hundred twenty delegates were elected in November 1970 to rewrite the Philippine Constitution. Well-known politicians, former presidents Diosdado Macapagal and Carlos P. Garcia, and other noted citizens were elected to the convention. Upon the insistence of student groups, the election of delegates was regulated by limiting campaign expenditures and by prohibiting elected and appointive officials currently in office from running for a seat in the convention. Partisanship was criticized, but the criticism did not prevent Marcos from releasing pork-barrel funds in the amount of 16,500 pesos to each Nacionalista congressman before the election of delegates on November 10.[21]

Many Filipinos had high hopes for the convention as "a cure-all for the ills facing the Philippines without realizing that many of the country's problems stem not from bad laws but from the selective enforcement or non-enforcement of adequate laws," according to Robert Tilman.[22] A similar sentiment was expressed by Claude Buss: "No one could see how a mere change in institutional framework could rectify a calamitous situation rooted in spiritual bankruptcy and corruption. No constitution deliberately violated could guarantee good government."[23]

The Constitutional Convention was opened at the Fiesta pavilion of the historic Manila Hotel on June 12, 1971. (The convention later moved its deliberations to the city hall of Quezon City.) Former president Garcia was elected as its presiding officer but because of his untimely death, Garcia was replaced by former president Macapagal, Marcos's predecessor.

The issue that occupied the convention was the form of government. Proposals for the creation of a parliamentary government argued that it suited Philippine society and politics better than the presidential system. The argument was not completely new to Philippine politics. The constitution of the first Philippine Republic (1899), often referred to as the Malolos Constitution, prescribed a parliamentary government with a fused executive-legislative branch and with the legislative branch having more power than the executive.[24]

The delegates, however, opposed a parliamentary government because Marcos would again be able to seek the presidency or the prime ministership as a representative or as a member of parliament. Marcos's constitutional term was to expire by December 31, 1973, and by virtue of the 1935 Constitution, he was not eligible for reelection because he would have already served two terms. Observers believed that Marcos was "unwilling to abandon power at the end of his second term . . . and wanted the constitutional convention [now] in session to either draft a new constitution to extend his term or remove the ban on three-term presidency."[25]

It was already July 1972, and the convention had completed only half of its task. Marcos's intentions to extend his term had been a constant threat to the convention. Another proposal was for Imelda Marcos to seek the presidency just in case Marcos were barred from doing so. As a response to the discussion on the matter of the Marcoses, 163 of the 311 delegates signed a petition barring Marcos, former presidents, including their spouses, or any of their close relatives by consanguinity or affinity within the fourth civil degree to run for the presidency or prime ministership. The proposal, however, failed to carry.[26]

By July 1972, after almost a year, with a vote of 158 to 120, the convention voted for a parliamentary government. It "would not have been predicted" the year before, "for although the issues have been raised, it was felt not to have wide support among the delegates." After the vote, a scandal rocked the convention. Convention delegate and former ambassador Eduardo Quintero, from the province of Leyte—Mrs. Marcos's province—revealed that he had received bribes on eighteen different occasions. Quintero said that the bribes came from Mrs. Marcos in order to influence the voting on presidential tenure or the form of government in the favor of the Marcoses. Quintero alleged that the bribery happened in meetings at Malacanang Palace. In what would be called the "payola scandal," the one who exposed the wrongdoing, Quintero, would himself be discredited. Charges were brought against him.[27] Primitivo Mijares, a Marcos assistant who later defected to the United States and testified before the Frazer Committee in the U.S. Congress, revealed that he himself was involved in propaganda to "de-glamorize" Quintero. Mijares, together with other presidential assistants, had gone to Leyte to gather "Quintero's dirt."[28] The convention's Committee on Privileges investigated the expose, and, by a vote of five to four declared the charge baseless.

PROCLAMATION 1081

In light of the unreliable performance of the delegates, on the evening of
September 23 Marcos made a statement over nationwide television and radio, which
had recently been taken over by the military. The president acknowledged that on
September 21 he issued Proclamation 1081 to put the entire country under martial
law. He said that he ordered the implementation of the proclamation at nine o'clock
in the evening of September 22. He said that the attempted ambush of Defense
Secretary Juan Ponce-Enrile was the immediate impetus for the proclamation.[29]
Marcos cited Article VII, Section 10, Paragraph 2 of the Philippine Constitution,
the legal and constitutional basis for the proclamation:

The president shall be Commander-in-Chief of all the Armed Forces of the Philippines,
and, whenever it becomes necessary he may call out such Armed Forces to prevent or
suppress lawless violence, invasion, insurrection, or rebellion. In case of invasion,
insurrection, or rebellion or imminent danger thereof, when the public safety requires it,
he may suspend the privilege of the writ of habeas corpus, or place the Philippines, or any
part thereof under martial law.

In Proclamation 1081, several threats to national security were cited as
justifications for using the president's emergency powers as commander-in-chief of
the armed forces. To show the existence of rebellion and the conditions provided for
in the Philippine Constitution, Marcos cited the Supreme Court's decision in 1971
upholding the legality of the suspension of the writ of habeas corpus. As discussed
previously, immediately after the bombing of the opposition party rally at Plaza
Miranda, Marcos suspended the right of the writ of habeas corpus through
Proclamation No. 889. It was amended nine days later by Proclamation 889-A, "to
bring it properly into line with Section 1 of the Bill of Rights as well as Section 10
of Article VII of the Constitution."[30]
The suspension was then lifted province by province, reducing the number of
areas where the proclamation was in force. On January 11, 1972, the right of the
writ of habeas corpus was restored. Judging by the Marcos government's actions,
then, conditions for the justification of suspending the writ of habeas corpus and for
the imposition of martial law no longer existed. If conditions for restoring the writ
of habeas corpus no longer existed, neither did the conditions for the existence of
martial law because according to the Philippine Constitution the conditions had to
be the same. The bombing at Plaza Miranda had been an immediate impetus for the
suspension of the writ, yet, a year after the bombing, the Marcos government had
not presented any evidence showing exactly who was responsible for the crime but
had simply charged the Communists with the deed. Proclamation 1081 also
mentioned the existence of violent confrontations between the government and
so-called subversives. It must be remembered that private armies did exist as
bodyguards of wealthy landowners, businesspeople, and politicians. Those private
armies fought each other, often as a result of conflicts between leaders or patrons.
The proclamation further cited violence on the island of Mindanao, which had
persisted for centuries. The Spaniards' attempts to convert the Muslims to Christ-

ianity and their plunder of the rich resources of Mindanao were the origins of that never-ending violence. Even during the American colonial era, fighting persisted in Mindanao. The newly independent Philippine government inherited the problem. Suspicion, borne of differences in religion, culture, social opportunities, and access to government, aggravated the situation. The holders of power merely paid lip service to integration and to giving more opportunities to Muslims. The influx of immigrants from Luzon and Visayas Islands brought more enmity. Government neglect and poverty brought about the "Mindanao problem," which, as some people from Mindanao said, was their "problem with the national government based in Manila." If the Mindinao problem was a reason for martial law, then the entire island should have been in a state of unceasing emergency.

There was also the New People's Army, the armed branch of the Communist Party of the Philippines that reorganized its forces in 1969. Socialist and communist groups had existed in the Philippines since the 1930s. The Huk movement attained the height of its power and was subsequently crushed in the 1050s. The organization persisted; but during the time of martial law, it was not strong enough to threaten the established government.

Proclamation No. 1081 also mentioned the shipment of arms in the months of May, June, and July 1972, introduced at Digoyo Point, Palanan, Isabela (a remote part of the eastern Pacific rim of the Philippines). It was alleged that the shipment included armaments and war materials such as M-14 rifles and several dozen 40mm rocket launchers "said to be Chicom [Chinese Communist] copies of a Russian prototype rocket launcher," rockets, and other ammunitions. The sources of those war materials were not identified. Marcos and his sources alluded to the Communists, but from what group or country, it was not clear. The arms shipment is still shrouded in mystery. The insularity of the Philippines and its separation from the mainland of Asia seem to be a barrier to the infusion of such aid, if ever such was possible, especially from the Pacific side of the archipelago. Although Philippine revolutionaries were inspired by Maoist-Leninist thought, Philippine radicalism and communism were homegrown. Rebellion was fertilized by unjust land tenure in Central Luzon and blossomed with Philippine nationalism.

Marcos cited these "security" reasons to give credence to his seizure of power. In fact, throughout the martial law years, the Marcos government used "red scare" tactics to justify and legitimize its rule. In 1984, without bowing to pressure from the opposition, Marcos stated that he needed to retain his decree powers in spite of the existence of a legislature "to allow a 'calibrated' response to the Communist insurgency," which ironically grew in terms of strength and sympathy because of the repressiveness of Marcos's authoritarian rule. His justifications became a self-fulfilling prophecy.

The response of the United States, giving aid to a supposedly anti-Communist dictator, also lent legitimacy to martial law. Given the repressiveness of the Marcos regime, which gained further strength from American support, the sympathy for rebel movements did increase among the peasantry and the intellectuals, and even among the urban dwellers and the small middle class.

THE MARCOS CONSTITUTION

The Constitutional Convention had been convening for almost sixteen months when martial law was imposed. After the imposition of martial law, some convention delegates were incarcerated or threatened with imprisonment. The deliberations of the Constitutional Convention became a mystery to many people, a direct result of censorship and control of the media by the Marcos government. For sixteen months before martial law, the convention was plagued with controversies about the form of government the Philippines should adopt. The convention was also rocked by scandals and was never free from the politicking of partisan politics. The process of drafting a constitution after imposition of martial law was, to use the words of Justice Robert Concepcion, "speeded up." By November 29, 1972, the Constitutional Convention approved a draft constitution.[31]

The proposed constitution provided for a parliamentary government. According to the 1935 Constitution, the president was the head of government and state and was popularly elected, but in the new constitution the president was just the ceremonial head of state elected from among the members of parliament.[32]

The legislative branch of government was to be a unicameral national assembly elected by district or apportionments of provinces, towns, and cities, as provided by law.[33] Both the president and the parliament were to be elected for six-year terms. From among its members the national assembly was to elect a prime minister who would then head the government. The prime minister would appoint a cabinet to execute the laws. The majority of the members of the cabinet or ministers would be appointed from among the members of the national assembly.[34] The proposed constitution also provided for a bill of rights as well as for an article of duties and obligations of citizens.[35] The voting age was lowered from twenty-one to eighteen.[36]

Despite martial law restrictions, misgivings about the new government were expressed, especially about the transitional provisions.[37] It provided for the formation of an interim national assembly that was to give priority to the orderly transition from the presidential to the parliamentary system, the reorganization of Government, the eradication of graft and corruption, the effective maintenance of peace and order, the implementation of declared agrarian reforms, the standardization of compensation of government employees, and such measures as shall bridge the gap between the rich and the poor.[38]

What was especially being questioned in the document was the composition of the interim National Assembly. According to Article XVII, Section 2:

The Members of the interim National Assembly shall be the incumbent President and Vice-President of the Philippines, those who served as President of the nineteen hundred and seventy-one Constitutional Convention, those Members of the Senate and the House of Representatives who shall express in writing to the Commission on Elections within thirty days after the ratification of this Constitution their option to serve therein and those Delegates to the nineteen hundred and seventy-one Constitutional Convention who have opted to serve therein by voting affirmatively for this article. They may take their oath of office before any officer authorized to administer oath and quality thereto, after the ratification of this Constitution.

Critics of the provision warned that incumbents wanted to perpetuate and prolong their service to their advantage, especially because there was no time limit on when the interim National Assembly should call for elections of the regular National Assembly. Critics also said that with Marcos pressuring the Constitutional Convention to finish a draft document, it had to be palatable to the Constitutional Convention delegates. It was said that the reward for Constitutional Convention delegates was the assurance that they would be representatives in the parliament. The interim National Assembly could also amend the proposed constitution with a vote of three-fourths of its members. The ratification of the amendment would be by the majority of votes cast in a plebiscite to be held not later than three months after the revision or approval of such amendment.[39] Members of Congress would not be disenfranchised, so their support was also expected for the proposed method of amending the new constitution.

The incumbent president, who was Ferdinand Marcos, was designated to convene the National Assembly. He was allowed to exercise the powers and duties vested by the new constitution, of both the president and the prime minister, and to enjoy such powers and exercise such duties until he called upon the interim National Assembly to elect the interim president and the interim prime minister.[40]

Section 3, Paragraph 2, legitimized the martial law decrees, orders and instructions, proclamations, and acts of President Marcos. It stated:

All proclamations, orders, decrees, instructions, and acts promulgated, issued or done by the incumbent President shall be part of the law of the land, and shall be valid, legal, binding, and effective even after lifting of martial law or the ratification of this Constitution, unless modified, revoked, or superseded by subsequent proclamations, orders, decrees, instructions, or other acts of the incumbent President, or unless expressly and explicitly modified or repealed by the regular National Assembly.

Not only were the above provisions questioned but so was the entire process of ratification, or the lack thereof. After the constitution was submitted to Marcos, he issued Presidential Decree No. 73 providing for the submission of the document to the Filipinos for ratification or rejection in a plebiscite to be held on January 15, 1973. The plebiscite was to be supervised by the Commission on Elections pursuant to the Election Code of 1971. General Order No. 17 was issued by Marcos, temporarily lifting "the effects of martial law" in order to allow free and open debate on the proposed constitution. A week after Marcos called for the plebiscite, petitioners filed a complaint with the Commission on Elections. They charged that Marcos did not have the power to call a plebiscite. Such power was vested in Congress alone as provided for in the 1935 Constitution. Several cases were filed before the Supreme Court: G.R. Nos. L-35925, 35929, 35940, 35941, 35942, 35948, 35953, 35965, and 35979.[41] The cases were heard on December 18 and 19. To sidestep a potentially embarrassing ruling by the court, on December 23, Marcos announced the indefinite postponement of the plebiscite and through General Order No. 20 rescinded the earlier permission for open and free debate. Marcos argued that the plebiscite had to be postponed because "a longer period was necessary to prepare the citizenry and to inform them thoroughly about the Constitution."[42] He issued Presidential Decree No. 90, which prohibited and punished as a crime "rumor mongering and spreading false information." By imposing that decree, he clamped down on and further discouraged any free discussion because any discussion or debate could be interpreted as rumor mongering. By issuing Letter of Instruction No. 11, Marcos served warning to the judiciary. In that letter, Marcos exempted himself from the pale of legal inquiry into the following: (1) questions involving the validity, legality, or constitutionality of Proclamation No. 1081 "or of any decree, or acts issued, promulgated or performed by me, or by my duly designated representative pursuant thereto"; and (2) questions involving the "validity, legality, or constitutionality of any rules, orders or acts issued and promulgated or performed by public servants pursuant to decrees, orders, rules and regulations issued and promulgated by me or by my duly designated representative pursuant to Proclamation No. 1081."

To avoid the legal issues of the plebiscite altogether, Marcos attempted to create a new means to give the new Philipine Constitution legitimacy. On December 31, 1972, he issued Presidential Decree Nos. 86, 86-A, and 86-B creating Citizens' Assemblies or *barangays*. *Barangays* corresponded to villages or barrios, the smallest political unit. The word *barangay* came from the pre-Hispanic name for groupings of people in villages. Historical accounts said that the word was synonymous with the word for *boat*, which was used to describe the mythical migration of Filipinos from other parts of Asia. The Citizens' Assemblies that were convened were loosely organized. There was no official registration of participants, nor were minutes of the meetings taken. Even those who were just fifteen years of age were allowed to participate in the deliberations. Local leaders herded groups of people into schoolhouses and other public places for meetings that were held on various dates between January 1 and January 15, 1973. The Marcos government claimed that such consultations were held in many areas; however, the claim is questionable. Deliberations might have been held in some areas, but in others, supposed results were reported only by the controlled mass media. Whatever the case, the following questions were asked in the said consultations:

1. Do you approve of the Citizens' Assembly as a way of popular government to decide issues affecting our people?

2. Do you approve of the new Constitution?

3. Do you want a plebiscite to be called to ratify the new Constitution?

4. Do you want to hold elections in November 1973 provided for in the 1935 Constitution?

5. If the election in 1973 is not held, when do you want the next elections to be called?[43]

6. Do you think Congress should meet again in regular session? Or do you like Congress to hold sessions again?

7. Do you like the way President Marcos is running the affairs of government?

8. Do you like the reforms under martial law?

9. Do you like the New Society?

Appended to those questions were the following suggested answers:

"The vote of the Citizens' Assemblies should be considered the plebiscite on the new Constitution."

"If the Citizens' Assemblies approve of the new Constitution, then the new Constitution should be deemed ratified."

"We do not want the ad interim National Assembly to be convoked at all, or, if it should be convoked at all, it should not be done until after at least seven years from the approval of the new Constitution by the Citizens' Assemblies."

The consultations took place outside the supervision of the constitutional body in charge of elections, the Commission on Elections. The consultations were directly supervised by the Office of the President and the Department of Local Government as well as Marcos's assistants. The executive branch, which should have been excluded from any form of election supervision, reported an overwhelming vote for the new Constitution. Ballots were not used. There was only a show of hands. Consultation results were published and became the basis for proclaiming the new Philippine Constitution.

After the establishment of the *barangays* or the Citizens' Assemblies, the effects of martial law were put in place again, and public discussion outside the assemblies was prohibited. The president declared that the people were "backsliding." "Backsliding" referred to a reversion to "old ways" that were contrary to the reforms envisioned in the New Society. The establishment of the Citizens' Assemblies was Marcos's response to the attempt of the members of Congress to fulfill their Constitutional obligations to convene that January. They were called upon by the Senate president, Gil Puyat, with the intention of convening Congress on January 22, 1973, so that they could call the plebiscite as was provided for by the 1935 Constitution.

It was not yet clear how the tallies and counts were made nor how deliberations were conducted. The entire exercise was also held without complying with the provisions of the Election Code. A certain person named Mr. Francisco Cruz, who was purported to be the president of the National Federation of Citizens' Assemblies, certified the overwhelming vote of 95% of the Filipinos in the assemblies in favor of the new Constitution. Chief Justice Robert Concepcion, however, in a Supreme Court resolution wrote:

The record shows that Mr. Cruz (the one who certified the results) had not even been a member of a *barrio* council since 1972, so that he could not possibly have been a member on January 17, 1973, of a municipal association of presidents of *barrio* or ward citizens' assemblies, much less of a provincial, city, or National Association or Federation of Presidents of any such provincial or city associations.

. . . Indeed, I cannot in good conscience, declare that the proposed Constitution has been approved or adopted by the people in the citizens' assemblies all over the Philippines, when it is, to my mind, a matter of judicial knowledge that there have been no such citizens' assemblies in many parts of the Philippines.[44]

Using the results of the deliberations of the Citizens' Assemblies, Marcos nonetheless proclaimed the ratification of the new Constitution by Proclamation 1102 on January 17, 1973.

In the proclamation, Marcos stated that 14,976,561 members of Citizens' Assemblies favored the adoption of the new Constitution and 743,869 rejected it. He further declared that 14,298,814 responded that there was no need for a plebiscite and that the vote of the Citizens' Assemblies considered its vote equivalent to the plebiscite. As the proclamation stated: "95 per cent of the members of the *barangays* (citizens' assemblies) [were] in favor of the new Constitution, so the *Katipunan ng mga Barangay* [had] strongly recommended that the new Constitution already be deemed ratified by the Filipino people." Marcos thus proclaimed the adoption of the new Constitution.[45]

The independence of the Supreme Court had been limited by Marcos, and as a result the court usually complied with his wishes. Various cases were brought before the Supreme Court about the ratification of the new Constitution, and those cases provided no exception to the Court's pattern of compliance. In *Planas v. Commission on Elections*, the plaintiff argued that the president did not have the authority to call a plebiscite,so it could not constitutionally be held because of the lack of free expression under martial law. The case was not decided. In actuality, a plebiscite was not held; there was, rather, a show of hands. The provision for constitutional amendments was not followed.

Several senators and others petitioned before the Supreme Court to prevent the executive from implementing the new Constitution or its provisions "on the ground that it had not been validly ratified and that it had not come into force and effect." They held that the purported referendum was irregular.[46]

Lawyer Joker Arroyo, representing Eduardo Monteclaro, the president of the National Press Club, stated that Citizens' Assemblies were "loose consultative bodies" and "sounding boards." Lawyer Raul Gonzalez argued that the assemblies' votes were reported hastily and much more rapidly than the results of regular elections. It took two weeks to report the results of regular elections, he said, whereas the results of the Citizens Assemblies' deliberations were reported in only twenty-four hours.[47] Lorenzo Tañada, former nationalist senator and civil rights leader, pointed out that the assemblies were held in an atmosphere of fear and the reports were falsely reported.[48] Tañada and other petitioners to the Supreme Court also claimed that the Department of Local Government "fabricated and misrepresented the results." In two provinces alone, the number of participants in the assemblies exceeded the number of registered voters by a million.[49] Solicitor-General Estelito Mendoza, arguing for the Marcos government, said there was "substantial compliance" to the provisions of the 1935 Constitution and denied the allegations of Tañada.[50]

Senator Jovito R. Salonga, acting as lawyer for his four colleagues in the Senate, "asked the Court not to give a judicial imprimatur to the kind of loose referendum of January but to uphold the old Constitution and pave the way for holding a 'genuine plebiscite' on the new Constitution."[51]

Chief Justice Robert Concepcion wrote a summary decision, a resume of votes cast, and the court's resolution, however, other justices also expressed their respective opinions, approach, and whatever they deemed as related issues and relevant cases, as well as priorities, qualifications, and modifications.

The justices agreed that the following questions related to the basic issues.

1. Is the issue of the validity of Proclamation No. 1102 a justiciable, or political and therefore non-justiciable, question?

2. Has the Constitution proposed by the 1971 Constitutional Convention been ratified validly, (with substantial, if not strict, compliance) conformable to the applicable constitutional and statutory provisions?

3. Has the aforementioned proposed Constitution been approved (with or without valid ratification) by the people?

4. Are petitioners entitled to relief? And,

5. Has the aforementioned proposed Constitution been put into force?[52]

The summary responses of the Supreme Court follow:

1. Regarding the political issue, six members of the court—Justices Makalintal, Zaldivar, Castro, Fernando, Teehankee, and Chief Justice Concepcion—held that the issue of the validity of Proclamation No. 1102 presents a justifiable and non-political question. Justices Makalintal and Castro did not vote directly on the question but only inferentially in their discussion of the second question. Justice Barredo qualified his vote, stating that inasmuch as it is claimed that there [had] been approval by the people, the Court may inquire into the question of whether or not there [had] actually been such approval, and, in the affirmative, the Court should keep its hands off approach out of respect for the people's will, but in the negative, the Court may determine from both factual and legal considerations whether or not Article XV of the 1935 Constitution [had] been complied with. Justices Makalintal, Antonio and Esguerra, or three members of the Court, held that the issue is political and beyond the ambit of judicial inquiry.

2. Regarding the validity of the ratification, Justices Makalintal, Zaldivar, Castro, Fernando, Teehankee, and the Chief Justice—or six members of the Supreme Court—also held "that the Constitution proposed by the 1971 Constitutional Convention was not validly ratified in accordance with

Article XV, Section 1 of the 1935 Constitution, which provides only one way for ratification, i.e., in an election or plebiscite held in accordance with law and participated in only by qualified and duly registered voters." Justice Barredo qualified his vote, stating that as to whether or not the 1973 Constitution has been validly ratified pursuant to Article XV, I still maintain that in the light of traditional concepts regarding the meaning and intent of said Article, the referendum in the Citizens' Assemblies, especially in the manner the votes therein were cast, reported and canvassed, falls short of the requirements thereof. In view, however, of the fact that I have no means of knowing to recognize as a judge that factually there was voting and that the majority of the votes were for considering approved the 1973 Constitution without the necessity of the usual form of plebiscite followed in past ratifications, I am constrained to hold that, in the political sense, if not in the orthodox legal sense, the people may be deemed to have cast their favorable votes in the belief that in doing so they did the part required of them by Article XV, hence, it may be said that in its political aspect, which is what counts most, after all, said Article has been substantially complied with, and, in effect, the 1973 Constitution has been constitutionally ratified. Justices Makasiar, Antonio, and Esguerra, or three members of the Court, held that in their view there has been in effect substantial compliance with the Constitutional requirements for valid ratification.

3. On the third question of acquiescence by the Filipino people in the aforementioned proposed Constitution, no majority vote has been reached by the Court." Four of its members—Justices Barredo, Makasiar, Antonio, and Esguerra—held that "the people have already accepted the 1973 Constitution." Two members of the Court, namely, Justice Zaldivar and the Chief Justice, [held] that there can be no free expression, and there has been no expression, by the people qualified to vote all over the Philippines, of their acceptance or repudiation of the proposed Constitution under Martial Law. Justice Fernando state[d] that '[if] it is conceded that the doctrine stated in some American decisions to the effect that independently of the validity of the ratification, a new Constitution once accepted or acquiesced to by the people must be accorded recognition by the Court, I am not at this stage prepared to state that such doctrine calls for application in view of the shortness of time that has elapsed and the difficulty of ascertaining what is the mind of the people in absence of freedom of debate that is a concomitant feature of martial law.' Three members of the Court expressed their lack of knowledge and/or competence to rule on the question. Justices Makalintal and Castro were joined by Justice Teehankee in their statement that "under a regime of martial law, with the free expression of opinions through the usual media vehicles restricted, they have no means of knowing, to the point of judicial certainty, whether the people have accepted the Constitution."

4. On the question of relief, six members of the court—Justices Makalintal, Castro, Barredo, Makasiar, Antonio and Esguerra—voted to dismiss the petition. Justices Makalintal and Castro so voted on the strength of their view that "the effectivity of the said Constitution, in the final analysis, is

the basic and ultimate question posed by these cases to resolve which considerations other than judicial, and therefore beyond the competence of this court, are relevant and unavoidable." Four members of the court—Justices Fernando, Teehankee, and Fernando and the Chief Justice—"voted to deny respondents' motion to dismiss and to give due course to the petitions."

5. Whether the new Constitution was in force, four members of the court—Justices Antonio, Barredo, Esguerra, and Makasiar—held that "it is in force by virtue of the people's acceptance thereof." Four other justices—Makalintal, Castro, Fernando, and Teehankee—did not cast a vote on the question or they abstained "on the premise stated in their votes on the third question that they could not state with judicial certainty whether the people have accepted or not accepted the Constitution." Two members of the court—Justice Zaldivar and the Chief Justice—voted that the Constitution proposed by the 1971 Constitutional Convention is not in force.

The Supreme Court's decision concluded:

Accordingly, by virtue of the majority of six votes of Justices Makalintal, Castro, Barredo, Makasiar, Antonio and Esguerra with four dissenting votes of the Chief Justice and Justices Zaldivar, Fernando, and Teehankee, all the aforementioned cases are hereby dismissed. This being the vote of the majority, *there is no further judicial obstacle to the New Constitution being in force and effect* (my emphasis).

The court, faced with a fait accompli, decided that no further judicial obstacle remained to putting the new Constitution into force. Government lawyers argued that the courts should not intervene in a delicate political situation, and the Supreme Court seemed to have heeded the advice by using vague language in its decision. Salonga pleaded that "courts worthy of the name are precisely erected to settle disputes. The more critical and difficult the situation, the greater the duty to make a redemptive contribution, according to our best lights and the dictates of our conscience."[53]

In Solicitor General Estelito Mendoza's argument, the court had to bow to the judgment of the people, as expressed through the Citizens' Assemblies. The Solicitor General stated, "The new Constitution having come into force, the court must now abide by popular judgment and accept the new charter as the source of its authority." He considered the case political rather than judicial; thus, a court's invalidation of the proclamation of the new Constitution would constitute a judicial veto of the acts of the Filipino people. He argued further, "Whatever improprieties there might have been in the procedure for ratification cannot overcome the fact that the new Constitution has been approved, or acquiesced to by the people."[54]

A key question articulated by Joaquin Bernas was whether "the 1973 Constitution [was] a product of revision or revolution?" According to Melville Fuller Westin's "Political Questions" published in the *Harvard Law Review* (1924-25), a written constitution is susceptible to change in two ways: "by revolution, which implies action not pursuant to any provision of the constitution itself; and by revision, which implies action pursuant to some procedural provision in the constitution."

Senator Arturo Tolentino used the same line of argument when he responded on behalf of the Senate president Gil Puyat, and Jose Roy, the Senate president pro tempore Jose Roy, both of Marcos's ruling Nacionalista Party, when other colleagues in the Senate were seeking to compel the Senate president to hold sessions. Tolentino argued that a real revolution had taken place when Marcos imposed martial law in September 1972, so that revolution was in force during the proclamation of the new Constitution. About the imposition of an authoritarian government, Tolentino said, "The Marcos revolution was a real revolution, with the distinction that it was carried out without bloodshed. . . . This revolution can perhaps be regarded as having succeeded since it appear[ed] to have the support of the military and the acquiescence of the civilian population."[55]

He argued, further, that "while there may [have] been irregularities in the conduct of the citizens' assemblies, there was no proof that a majority did not, in fact, endorse President Marcos's martial law and the new Constitution."[56] Tolentino's argument was also reflected in Marcos's *Today's Revolution Democracy, Notes on the New Society*, and the other essays attributed to him. Marcos considered the issue raised before the Supreme Court as a question of the legitimacy of his entire government. He claimed to receive persistent suggestions "to proclaim a revolutionary government in the event of an adverse (Supreme Court) decision. But nevertheless, he submitted to the jurisdiction of the Court."[57]

It would not have mattered what decision the Supreme Court made because Marcos could ultimately have justified his actions by establishing a revolutionary government. In their final pleading, "petitioning lawyers asked the court to act decisively, quoting Justice Oliver Wendell Holmes's advice that to think great thoughts, you must be heroes as well as idealists." In its decision, the Supreme Court opted for pragmatism. To the petitioners it responded, "Justice Holmes addressed the phrase not to judges but to scholars and argued that the court should be 'pragmatists rather than idealists.'"[58]

Marcos had earned significant legal justification for his authoritarian regime. In his own words: "The new Constitution was a basis or foundation for the structure of law that would govern the New Society."[59] He pursued legitimacy through the constitution he claimed was the foundation of the structure of law, but that constitution would be selectively implemented, and further rethought through succeeding referendums and other political rituals. Rituals to justify the legitimacy of the authoritarian government were conducted from time to time and from crisis to crisis.

The United States continued its low key response to the proclamation of the 1973 Constitution as well as to the continuing trend "toward one-man rule in the Philippines by President Ferdinand E. Marcos," when he assumed powers as president, prime minister, and legislator.[60] Although Washington officials were reportly deeply concerned, when asked to comment on events in the Philippines, State Department spokesperson Charles W. Bray III said: "We have noted these developments, but I will have no comment on them."[61]

Once the new Constitution was in place and his position "legally" established, Marcos maintained the legal trappings of democracy. Elections and referendums were held under martial law. Like the show-of-hands "referendum" that approved the 1973 Constitution, however, these elections and referendums served as "democratic forms merely to legitimize authoritarian rule."[62]

REFERENDUMS

Referendums were held four times before the election for the 1978 Interim Batasang Pambansa in April 1978. In each case, Marcos tried to gain legitimacy for his rule through direct assent from the people, at the same time employing decidedly undemocratic tactics to ensure that the referendums returned the desired results. In the referendum of July 27-28, 1973, Filipino voters were asked if they wanted Marcos to continue as president beyond 1973 "to finish reforms he [had] initiated under martial law." Marcos's term of office under the 1973 Constitution would have ended by December 30, 1973.

Marcos extended to two days the voting originally scheduled for one day. He also decreed that registered voters who failed to vote would face up to six months imprisonment. Qualified voters who failed to register would be fined. The decrees pressured people into participating in the referendum. Voters were asked to write their comments about and expectations of the regime on an attached sheet of paper. After the first day of voting, the government announced that early results showed that the votes ran five to one in favor of martial law and the extension of Marcos's rule. Later it was reported that 90.61% of the voters had voted yes. The referendum gave no alternative to those voters who had voted no. There were many irregularities. Government officials pressured voters; even the Commission on Elections was not impartial.

Opposition to the regime manifested itself only through the underground media and the distribution of leaflets. For fear of reprisals, not many objected to or criticized the regime. The regime completely controlled the media. Salonga and other political, religious, and educational leaders denounced the referendum as "fictitious" and sent a letter of protest to Marcos.[63] They said that "martial law prevented the free exchange of ideas."

Even after winning the referendum of July 1973, Marcos announced another referendum for September 1974. He wanted to show that martial law had strong support in the Philippines. Postponed until January 1975, the referendum was not held until February 27, 1975.

The referendum posed the following questions:

1. Do you approve of the manner [in which] President Marcos has been exercising his powers under martial law and the constitution, including the power to issue proclamations, orders, decrees, and instructions with the force of law?

2. Do you want the President to continue exercising the same powers?[64] In Greater Manila it was asked whether the voters in four cities and

municipalities approved of an integrated form of government. Outside
Greater Manila it was asked whether after December 31, 1975, local
officials should be appointed by the president or elected.[65]

The terms of office for local officials would have ended December 31, 1975. The
approval of the provision making their positions appointive placed their tenure at the
discretion of the president. Local officials had to toe the line of the regime to
preserve their offices as well as their interests.

According to a noted Philippine observer: "Since the questions changed with the
dates, it seemed clear that the weather alone could not explain the delays." The
regime needed to legitimize itself before critics, who were growing restless and
vocal against martial law, as well as before the U.S. government, which dispensed
aid to the Philippines.[66]

Four bishops and thirteen social action directors from Mindanao dioceses
denounced the referendum. Bishops Francisco Claver of Bukidnon and Jesus Varela
of Ozamis both issued individual statements. Bishop Claver's letter to Marcos was
read in all pulpits of his parishes. He expressed approval of the boycott of the
referendum.[67]

Fourteen individuals, among them five Roman Catholic bishops and Senator
Benigno Aquino, filed a petition before the Supreme Court to bar Marcos from
calling the referendum. They charged that Marcos did not have the authority to call
a referendum because he did not hold office legally. Three weeks before the
referendum, the case was heard in court. Marcos was ruled president "in fact as
well as by law."[68]

In *Aquino et al. v. Comelec*,[69] the Philippine Supreme Court decided unani-
mously that the present government of the Philippines was a de jure government and
that President Marcos was its de jure president, with the right to continue office
even beyond his second term, which expired on December 30, 1973, by virtue of
the transitional provision of the new Constitution.[70]

As the basis for its ruling, the Supreme Court cited the results of the previous
referendum as well as the 1973 Constitution. The court ruled that under the 1935
Constitution, President Ferdinand E. Marcos was duly re-elected by the vote of the
sovereign people in the presidential elections of 1969 by an overwhelming vote of
over 5,000,000 electors as against 3,000,000 for his rival, garnering a majority of
about 896,498 to 1,436,118 (Osmena vs. Marcos, Presidential Election Contest No.
3, January 8, 1973). While his term of office under the 1935 Constitution should
have terminated on December 30, 1973, the sovereign people expressly authorized
him to continue in office even beyond 1973 under the 1973 Constitution (which was
validly ratified on January 17, 1973 by the sovereign people) in order to finish the
reforms he initiated under Martial Law; and as aforestated, as this was the decision
of the people, in whom 'sovereignty resides xxx and all government authority
emanates xxx,' it is therefore beyond the scope of judicial inquiry (*Aquino, Jr. v.
Enrile et al.* 242). The logical consequence therefore is that President Marcos is a
de jure President of the Republic of the Philippines.[71]

In spite of the ruling, Filipinos took to the streets to protest the referendum. Five thousand people marched and chanted revolutionary songs. The protest grew out of a four-hour religious procession and was the first big antigovernment rally since martial law had been imposed. Former Senator Tañada called for a boycott. He was joined by the Association of Major Religious Superiors (AMRS). The Catholic Bishops Conference also supported the boycott and "called on Marcos to eliminate criminal penalties against boycotters to provide safeguards to make the referendum meaningful."[72] The bishops stated that a meaningful referendum required "free public discussion, freedom of speech, of peaceful assembly and of all media; a non-partisan, reputable, body of three citizens to conduct and supervise the referendum; and the suspension of penalties on those who fail to vote or abstain from voting."[73]

Even if the government acquiesced to these requirements, however, the religious people, according to the Catholic Bishops Conference, will remain unconvinced because "they have deep-seated, conscientious objections to the forthcoming referendum. Those who . . . follow their conscience to the extent of being ready to suffer for it deserve respect however much we may disagree with their views . . . [for] in all his activity, man is bound to follow his conscience."[74]

Marcos campaigned despite not giving any alternative to Filipino voters except his statement that if the people voted no to the continuation of his regime, the government would "return to a parliamentary system." His promise was empty, however, because the parliamentary system had never been implemented in the Philippines.

A few days before the referendum, Primitivo Mijares, a leading Marcos assistant who called himself chief censor and propagandist, defected to the United States and sought asylum. He said, "I can no longer risk my neck for a government that is taking care of only the economic requirements of the in-laws of the leader and his cronies."[75] Among other things, Mijares testified before a U.S. congressional committee that the results of the first referendum were falsified with his help together with that of other assistants of Marcos. Mijares said he orchestrated a media event to make it appear that a referendum overwhelmingly approving the 1973 Constitution took place.[76] Mijares said that Marcos—"the dictator"—imposed martial law because "he never intended to relinquish power." He asserted that he himself "personally participated in the fabrication of the results of the January 1973 and July 1973 referendums." The February referendum, he said, would be rigged and that Marcos would gain 90% support.[77]

Mijares's predictions proved right: Ninety percent of the electorate "approved the manner in which President Marcos had been exercising his powers under Martial Law and the Constitution including the power to issue proclamations, orders, decrees and instructions with the force of law" and that Marcos continued to exercise the same powers.[78]

Likewise Marcos was authorized to appoint "the successors of local elective officials whose terms of office expire on December 31, 1975" and "to restructure the local government in Greater Manila into an integrated system like a manager or commission form under such terms and conditions as he may decide."[79]

Through Presidential Decree Nos. 991 and 1033, dated September 2 and 22, 1976, respectively, Marcos called for a "referendum-plebiscite" on October 16, 1976. Once more the voters were asked if they approved of martial law and if they wanted it continued. In addition, a set of amendments to the Philippine Constitution was proposed. It included Amendment Six, which granted the president legislative powers in spite of his plan to convene a legislature.

The following amendments were proposed:

1. There shall be, in lieu of the interim National Assembly, an Interim *Batasang Pambansa* (IBP). Members of the Interim *Batasang Pambansa*, which shall not be more than 120, unless otherwise provided by law, shall include (1) the incumbent President of the Philippines, (2) representatives elected from different regions of the nation, (3) those who shall not be less than eighteen years of age, elected by their respective sectors in accordance with the number of their respective inhabitants, and (4) members of the Cabinet appointed by the President. Regional representatives shall be apportioned among the regions in [proportion to] the number of their respective inhabitants and on the basis of a uniform and progressive ratio while the sectors shall be determined by law. The number of representatives from each region or sector, and the manner of their election, shall be prescribed and regulated by law.

2. The Interim *Batasang Pambansa* shall have the same powers, and its members shall have the same functions, responsibilities, rights, privileges, and disqualifications as the interim National Assembly, the regular National Assembly, and the members thereof. [The Interim *Batasang Pambansa*,] however, it shall not exercise the power provided in Article VII, Section 14, (1) of the Constitution.

3. The incumbent President of the Philippines shall, within 30 days from the election and selection of the members, convene the Interim *Batasang Pambansa* and preside over its sessions until the Speaker shall have been elected. The incumbent President of the Philippines shall be the Prime Minister, and he shall continue to exercise all his powers even after the Interim *Batasang Pambansa* is organized and ready to discharge its functions, . . . likewise, he shall continue to exercise his powers and prerogatives under the 1935 Constitution and the powers vested in the President and the Prime Minister under [that] Constitution.

4. The President (Prime Minister) and his Cabinet shall exercise all the powers and functions, and discharge the responsibilities of the regular President (Prime Minister) and his cabinet, and shall be subject only to such disqualifications as the President (Prime Minister) may prescribe. The President (Prime Minister), if he so desires, may appoint a Deputy Prime Minister or as many Deputy Prime Ministers as he may deem necessary.

5. The incumbent President shall continue to exercise legislative powers until martial law shall have been lifted.

6. Whenever, in the judgment of the President (Prime Minister), there exists a grave emergency (or a threat or imminence thereof), or whenever the Interim *Batasang Pambansa* or the regular National Assembly fails to (or is unable to) act adequately on any matter for any reason [which the President believes] requires immediate action, [the President] may, [in order] to meet the exigency, issue the necessary decrees, orders, or letters of instructions, which shall form part of the law of the land.

7. The *barangays* and *sanggunians* shall continue as presently constituted, but their functions, powers, and composition may be altered by law. Referendums conducted through the *barangays* under the supervision of the Commission on Elections may be called at any time the government deems it necessary [in order] to ascertain the will of the people [on] any important matter whether of national or local interest.

8. All provisions of this Constitution inconsistent with any of these amendments shall continue in full force and effect.

9. These amendments shall take effect after the incumbent president shall have proclaimed that they have been ratified by a majority of votes cast in the referendum-plebiscite.[80]

As in previous referendums, Marcos let those aged fifteen and older participate in the referendum, while those who had the right to vote on the Constitution, eighteen years and older, were said to be participants in a plebiscite in amending the Constitution.

In an effort to prevent Marcos from calling that "referendum-plebiscite," which would further entrench his wide powers, several individuals filed cases in the Supreme Court to restrain the holding of the "referendum-plebiscite." Thousands of demonstrators, including priests and nuns, protested martial law and the "referendum-plebiscite." They ended by clashing with club-swinging police.[81] Various opposition groups conducted a boycott; however, as in the past, the Marcos regime proclaimed 90% approval of martial law as well as of the amendments to the Constitution.

In August 1977, with the convening of the *Batasang Pambansa*, there were discussions about retaining the presidential system or not. Marcos announced that he would like to seek reelection probably by the end of 1977. Later he said he would call a referendum in order to seek a mandate and hold *Batasang Pambansa* elections in May 1978; however, all those discussions ended in confusion and varying positions.[82]

As Marcos had announced during the *Batasang Pambansa* discussions, a referendum was held on December 17, 1977. The issue in that referendum was "whether Marcos should continue as President and also become Prime Minister after organization of the *Batasang Pambansa* (BP)." According to Marcos, an affirmative vote would "pave the way for the *Batasang Pambansa* according to his schedule," whereas if there was "a massive no vote he would resign as President, call elections for the *Batasang Pambansa*, and run for a seat in his home district."[83] Again came a call for boycott. The outcome was not far from the results of previous referendums. To the surprise of no one, Marcos reported an overwhelming 89.53% in favor of his proposal.[84]

Under martial law, Marcos used referendums as devices to legitimize his regime. For the regime to hold authority, it needed a mandate from the people. It created that through carefully orchestrated events. The media did not provide time or space for opposing views; thus, the critics of Marcos's tactics resorted to other means of protest. Religious leaders issued criticisms from the pulpits. Religious and civic leaders staged demonstrations and protests as well as campaigns to boycott the referendums. Although the referendums gave a semblance of democracy, the meaningful participation of citizens was impossible in a "managed affair to provide legitimacy to the martial law regime."[85] Because there were no guarantees to civil liberties, dissenters were subject to arrest and detention. Even nonparticipants faced possible prosecution and punishment.

Referendums provided a means of altering the Constitution to suit the needs of the circumstances and they paved the way for proclaming the 1973 Constitution; indefinitely extending Marcos's term, which should have expired by December 30, 1973; granting Marcos the power to appoint and remove local government officials, who thus served their tenure at Marcos's pleasure; integrating the municipalities and city governments in Greater Manila, thus paving the way for Mrs. Marcos's appointment as governor; creating the *Batasang Pambansa,* a quasi-legislative body that many have called a "rubber-stamp" parliament; and making Marcos both president and prime minister.

ELECTIONS

Motivated by his concern for legality, Marcos called not only referendums but elections as well. After six years of martial law, Marcos decided that it would be good to hold an election. Surely an election under martial law would provide a touch of democracy. Marcos mentioned "normalization" and even the possibility of a presidential election as well as the lifting of martial law; however, he did not go so far as to call elections for the IBP as provided in the amendments to the Constitution placed before the electorate in the referendum of 1976. Marcos took more than a year to implement the amendment about the IBP; but even with the creation of the *Batasan*, Marcos's decree powers continued. The structure of the IBP maintained power in the hands of Marcos. The IBP had no fixed term and could be dissolved by Marcos whenever he wished. It could not review his decrees nor overrule his veto. The structure of the IBP also favored the regime.[86]

Of 200 assemblymen, 165 were popularly elected from constituencies coincident with the twelve administrative regions and Metro Manila; fourteen were selected on a geographical basis by government-sponsored youth, agricultural, and labor organizations; and twenty-one were the prime minister and his appointees, chosen primarily from among the members of the cabinet.[87]

The announcement of the election for the IBP, scheduled in April 16, 1978, was met with skepticism. The leaders of the Liberal Party, Gerardo Roxas and Jovito

Salonga, denounced the election as a useless exercise.[88] They did not participate in the elections at all. Jose Diokno, who represented the Civil Liberties Union of the Philippines, also objected to the elections. He warned that by participating in the elections, one recognized the legitimacy of the regime. Benigno Aquino, in contrast, organized a slate of opposition candidates for Metro Manila. He campaigned and ran for office from his cell in Fort Bonifacio. He was running for office, he said, in order "to have the opportunity to talk to the Filipino people." He headed the LABAN party—"LABAN" means *fight* and is an acronym of Lakas ng Bayan ("Power of the People"). Other than some small groups in Visayas and Mindanao, that party was the only credible opposition to the regime's candidates.

Marcos organized the Kilusan ng Bagong Lipunan (KBL) ng mga Nacionalista, Liberal at Iba Pa (Party of Nationalists, Liberals, and Others), an umbrella party that included current government officials from the Liberal Party and the Nationalist Party who were coopted by the regime. Marcos's wife, Imelda, led the twenty-one candidates in Metro Manila. Marcos's own position as prime minister was assured in spite of the claims that this was a parliamentary system; thus Marcos did not run for a seat in his own province.

Forty-five days of campaigning were allowed during which some martial law restrictions were lifted. The media, however, were still completely controlled by the regime, so opposition candidates in Metro Manila resorted to campaigning personally. They also conducted and organized a noise campaign. Aquino was given the chance to speak and to be interviewed on television. He spoke eloquently when interviewed on the program Face the Nation, revealing that since 1973 he had been held mostly in solitary confinement and had been sentenced to death by firing squad.

Marcos focused his attacks on Aquino, citing his alleged connections with the CIA, thus diffusing the issues of the election. Marcos hoped also that his allegations would win the sympathy of Nationalists.

Marcos's control of the entire government was a formidable advantage. To assure the support of government employees, Marcos decreed new insurance and retirement benefits and increased the salaries of teachers.[89] Schoolteachers who took charge of the polling places were also given a pay increase of 100 pesos and "offered guarantees of 250,000 new homes."[90] Election rules favored the regime, especially the promulgation of "optional block voting." Voters could merely write the name of the party on the ballot, and the votes would automatically go to the entire ticket. Optional block voting also made ballots easier to alter or replace. If there was coercion, then electors could easily be forced to vote for one party, but coercion could be easily verified. Although legality of block voting was questioned in the Supreme Court, on March 11, 1978 the Supreme Court affirmed its legality.[91] The Supreme Court ruled that "party voting is time honored and historically precedented; the system is not violative of the equal protection clause in the Constitution, and optional party voting is consistent with free, orderly, and honest elections."[92] Since 1946, however, the Supreme Court had consistently turned down block voting.

The opposition was popular in Manila despite the advantages given to Marcos's KBL. Even though there were well-founded fears of cheating and fraud by government-sponsored candidates, some Filipinos hoped that at least a few opposition candidates would win in Metro Manila because their slate included former senators and congressmen who were already known to the voting public. Only in Manila and in a few parts of Viscayas and Mindanao did opposition candidates appear on the ballots. According to Carl Lande, an American political scientist who observed the elections:

It was apparent that the great majority of the city's people supported (the opposition) slate. Neighborhood rallies for the opposition were packed with members of the working and lower middle classes, who stood for hours to hear the candidates lambast the regime. Neighborhood rallies for the government candidates, on the other hand, drew much smaller numbers, mostly children and neighborhood riffraff who had been provided with chairs and sandwiches and, in some cases, had been paid to attend. Only when the government changed its tactics and bussed thousands of teenagers to rallies at central locations was it able to create the appearance of massive backing. The opposition sent out word to its sympathizers to show their support on the evening before election day by making noise, blowing horns or beating pans for 15 minutes. When the appointed time arrived the noise began, rose to the level of bedlam, and continued in various parts of the city for three to four hours.[93]

Lande was referring to the noise barrage of April 6. The appointed time was ten o'clock. Around that time shouts of "Ninoy" (Aquino's nickname) and "Laban" were heard. Noise blasted throughout the city. On first hearing the noise, one might think that noise was all there was to the protest. But crowds of people slowly gathered in the streets. Cars, bike riders, and a throng of paraders marched through the streets of Manila. There were firecrackers. People from all walks of life joined the protest in the streets.[94] The regime was so alarmed that imposed draconian measures after the elections.

The schedule of the election gave advantages to the KBL. It coincided with the Holy Week/Easter vacation of schools and universities. Students who were strong regime opponents were on vacation in their respective provinces and away from opposition politics in Manila; in contrast, government employees living in Manila were encouraged by Marcos "not to go home to their provinces to vote, but to go to Metro Manila polls." The KBL spokesperson, former ambassador to Egypt J. V. Cruz, announced that "Metro Manila residents who came from the northern Ilocos region, Marcos's homeland, and the islands of Leyte and Samar, Imelda Marcos's birthplace, could vote in the capital as there was no opposition contesting the election in these areas."[95]

Voter registration was extended up to two days before the election and continued until April 5; thus, the opposition would not have the time to challenge the registration of "flying voters." Even Marcos himself admitted that "there may have been election irregularities. . . . [T]he question was to what extent."[96] There were reports of ballot-box stuffing in some 11,500 voting precincts in Metro Manila. Some voters found ballot boxes already full just after the opening of polling places.

The supervision of the Commission on Elections, which was completely under the control of Marcos's appointees, made the whole process questionable. Their appointments to office were not subject to confirmation by the Committee on Appointments, a joint congressional committee that approved presidential appointees before the imposition of martial law. The members of the Commission on Elections' tenure of office, as well as that of their staff and employees, was thus subject to Marcos's control. Ballot counting was subject to police harassment and fraud. The returns came in slowly, arousing the suspicion of cheating. Marcos was quick to claim victory for his KBL.

Six hundred protesters were arrested in a large march of protest against the results and conduct of the election. Those arrested and put into prison included LABAN candidates: Teofisto Guingona, Francisco Rodrigo, Ernesto Rondon, and campaign manager Lorenzo Tañada. LABAN candidates Ernesto Maceda and Charito Planas fled to the United States and sought asylum there. Marcos said that he would not tolerate more protests or antigovernment activities. Foreign Minister Carlos P. Romulo, himself one of the KBL Metro Manila candidates, accused foreign media of inciting the protests and wrote to the U.S. state secretary, Cyrus Vance, claiming that the inciting actions constituted a danger to Philippine national security.[97]

Marcos threw back opposition charges of fraud. He turned things around and ridiculed the opposition as responsible for fraud. He insulted the losers and accused them of "sour grapes." Marcos controlled the media and put the opposition leadership in prison, so they could not even defend themselves.

On June 12, 1978, the interim IBP opened with the overwhelming majority of its members under the president's KBL. Only thirteen opposition candidates won. The thirteen were from the Pusyon Bisaya and Mindanao Alliance Parties from the southern Philippines. Their numbers were enough for Marcos to show that the opposition was represented. Presidential decrees, dated June 11, 1978, appeared regularly even after the opening of the *Batasan*, contrary to Marcos's claims that he would relinquish his legislative powers. Assemblyman Felimon Fernandez described June 11 as "the longest day" because of the numerous decrees written or presumed to have been written before the opening of the *Batasan*.[98]

Called a "rubber-stamp parliament," the *Batasan* was the object of many jokes. A popular columnist called it "an expensive Xerox copying machine."[99] Even some *Batasan* members themselves admitted to their ineffectiveness and poor performance. One member filed a resolution "urging the Prime Minister (Ferdinand E. Marcos) to advise the President of the Philippines (Ferdinand E. Marcos) on the Dissolution of the Interim Batasang Pambansa . . . for being a puppet parliament and a democratic facade for an authoritarian regime."[100]

The election and convening of the IBP was used by Marcos as an instrument for legitimizing his authoritarian regime. His party was for the most part unopposed. First, contesting elite clans and factions in various regions competed to run under the banner of the KBL to guarantee support and victory. Marcos stepped into local controversies to settle factional rivalries. In certain instances he remained neutral, allowing the rivals to fight among themselves and thereby keeping the political conflicts contained. After all, those competing factions would eventually seek government support and patronage.

At the minimum, LABAN candidates hoped to gain a stage for articulating opposing views. For them, the election was a chance to be heard or at least to rouse people's sentiments and awareness.[101] The inclusion of nontraditional politicians on the opposition slate, such as student leader Gerry Barican, labor leader Alex Boncayo, and Manila squatters' organizer Trinidad Herrera, signaled a shift in the orientation of electoral politics. Former senator Salonga commented: "This election may be a sham. I will say that, but it has awakened the slumbering sense of injustice of the people."[102]

Right after the election, Marcos proved himself in tight control with the arrest of hundreds of protesters and LABAN leaders. His show of force served as a reminder to those "awakened" by the election. Even the archbishop of Manila, Cardinal Jaime Sin, who was then classified not as a conservative, progressive, or liberal among Philippine bishops but as a fence-sitter, was placed on a travel ban list after the election. He had issued a pastoral letter urging an honest and fair election. At the Manila International Airport on his way to Rome for a synodal meeting, the cardinal learned that he would not be allowed to leave the country. Upon learning of the ban, the outraged cardinal remarked, "So, I am a subversive." Immediately he made a call to the presidential palace, and the "error" said to be caused by an overzealous military was rectified.[103] Thenceforth, however, there would be strain and tension in the relationship between the Marcos government and the cardinal.

Several priests and nuns stated that they were "convinced that widespread irregularities, some of them violative of human rights, characterized the last elections in the Metro Manila area." Two aides of Father Romeo Intengan, a Jesuit priest who himself was placed in prolonged detention, were tortured by the military while in their custody. One of them died. Despite the autopsy showing that Teotimo Tantiado was tortured, his military custodians were absolved.[104]

As one person interviewed by the author commented: "I don't believe that elections will cause change for the better. It is only a way for the regime to know who its friends and supporters are, as well as its enemies."

Not only did Marcos call national elections, but he allowed local ones as well. Since 1972, local officials had been serving at the pleasure of Marcos. Through the referendum in 1975, their positions were made appointive. Many provincial governors, town mayors, council members, down to the *barangay* captain, shifted their allegiance to the Marcos regime. They had to deal with his administration for survival; so they pragmatically joined and supported the KBL to be assured of patronage.[105]

Toward the end of 1979, Marcos surprised his opponents by scheduling local elections for January 30, 1980, not quite nine years after the last local elections. A number of people took his announcement with resignation rather than with excitement. Opposition leaders dismissed the election as "not so much an election, more of a selection," reminiscent of past referendums.[106] The sudden announcement of the elections did not give his opponents time to organize and left them with few resources and no access to the media.

Marcos immediately released funds for infrastructure building and project works. Every *barangay* leader was promised 5,000 pesos (US $685) for *barangay* projects.[107] Squabbles ensued in local areas for the sponsorship of the KBL, which Marcos formalized as a political party. Nacionalists, who wanted to be assured of full support became full-fledged KBL members. Those who did not were left to be the candidates of the Nacionalista or other parties. Marcos questioned those who remained as Nacionalistas because they were not chosen as official KBL candidates. He called them turncoats. Whoever was left from LABAN and Liberal Party did not participate in the elections. Instead, they just supported small ad hoc groups such as the National Union for Liberation (NUL). The Mindanao Alliance won two governorships and two mayoralty positions; however, the victories were extremely low compared to a sweeping fifty out of fifty-nine mayoralty seats for KBL. In the seventy-three provinces, sixty-eight elected governors were KBL. Among those who won in the local elections was Marcos's son, Ferdinand "Bongbong" Marcos, Jr. He was elected as vice-governor to his aunt, Elizabeth Marcos-Rocca, governor of Ilocos Norte.

In the province of Batangas, the Laurels and the Levistes, who were rivals, fought hard for the governorship. The Levistes received Marcos's support. For the Laurels, it was not only a local contest between them and the Levistes but also a contest between them and Marcos.

The election was disturbed by violence throughout the archipelago. Even Marcos himself acknowledged election irregularities: cheating, fraud, intimidation, and vote buying,[108] but he was quick to claim victory for his party. Voters were bussed to polling places, and "election-related" expenses were distributed to *barangay* officials for their constituents. In other instances, force was used to influence the outcome of the voting; for example, schoolteachers in charge of polling places were held at gunpoint during the counting of votes in the province of Pampanga.

Even Marcos-appointed Comelec chairman Vicente M. Santiago raised doubts about the adequacy of election laws in ensuring an honest election. The "flying voters" and illegal registrants were on voter rolls. If election laws were inequitable, the circumstances of the opposition heightened the inequity. The small opposition continued to be divided by personal rifts and ambitions and lack of resources, so opposition was fragile to nonexistent as party machinery. The incumbents, presumably enjoying Marcos's support in their extended seven-year term of office, had the advantage of patronage. Many people owed them favors. They could deliver and withdraw rewards. Their years of unchallenged incumbency strengthened their power bases, so the election legitimized beyond doubt the authority of Marcos and his allies. According to the *Far Eastern Economic Review*:

The situation seems to sit well with Marcos. The election proved beyond doubt the clout of the KBL under his absolute leadership. No opposition group appears to be in any position to challenge his leadership of government. Yet through the election he has been able to show that there exist opposition groups which can freely contest government candidates in popular elections.[109]

In a study of the evolution of Filipino political institutions, Raul de Guzman said: "For a martial law regime, elections are neither too serious an obstacle to overcome nor too difficult a concession to make." The battle for electoral positions was not going to be on an even keel because the power of the martial law regime was not limited. The regime had the power to make electoral rules and procedures, to place its own people in the Commission on Elections, to release the budget for offices, and development projects, and to persuade the media to its side. The Kilusang Bagong Lipunan (KBL) became the major, if not the only, political party to dominate whatever elections were conducted. The KBL afforded limited choice from among the candidates on its slate; for the people it became a matter of choice between voting for administration-supported KBL candidates or the weak opposition parties. Elections in the end did not turn out to be fair, honest, and decent competition among candidates for offices. The non-KBL candidates did not have an equal chance. The results of the elections were predictable: only KBL candidates won with a few exceptions. Elections became the legitimizing forum for the administration. It served the purpose of administration but failed in winnowing the qualified from the unfit.[110]

CONCLUSION

Through his use of fraudulent elections and referendums, Marcos established the precedent for setting aside democratic processes when they interfered with his authoritarian designs. Government energy shifted from the rational formulation of public policy to the pursuit of ways to satisfy his need for legitimacy. Above all, his legal maneuvers created political instability by weakening the force of constitutional law. The 1935 Constitution, which had provided stability, predictability, and peaceful change, was altered through amendments enacted through referendums. No longer was the Philippine Constitution a durable document for governance. The framework of government and democratic processes was made pliant by the frequent need of the authoritarian regime to claim its legitimacy.

As will be shown in the next chapter, the network of alliances of the civilian and military bureaucracy was tied to patron-client relationships and extended further to local politicians, businesspeople, and other beneficiaries of the authoritarian system, leading to an erosion of the standards of civil service and to the pervasive abuse of public office. Public bureaucracy was used for private gains and ends, such as the establishment of monopolies and the use of the public treasury for private functions and needs. Public officials blurred the boundaries between the public domain and the private domain. They overextended bureaucratic resources and time for patronage and image-building projects, thus increasing public spending and debt.

NOTES

1. James Madison, *Federalist* No. 47.
2. Speech of President Marcos during the Loyalty Day celebration, at Camp Aguinaldo, Quezon City, September 10, 1974, "A Pledge of Loyalty to the Republic," in Carolina G. Hernandez, "The Extent of Civilian Control of the Military in the Philippines, 1946-1976" (Ph.D. dissertation, State University of New York, Buffalo, 1979), p. 217.

3. U.S. Congress, Senate, Committee on Foreign Relations, *Korea and the Philippines, November 1972: A Staff Report for the Use of the Committee on Foreign Relations*, 93rd Cong., 1st sess., 1973, p. 2.

4. Primitivo Mijares, *The Conjugal Dictatorship of Ferdinand and Imelda Marcos I* (San Francisco: Union Square Publications, 1976).

5. *Time*, October 2, 1972, p. 34; *New York Times*, October 17, 1972, p. 6, and November 3, 1972, p. 6.

6. Mijares, *Conjugal Dictatorship*, p. 327.

7. Quoted in Mijares, ibid., p. 326. See David A. Rosenberg, "Liberty versus Loyalty: The Transformation of Philippine News Media under Martial Law," in David A. Rosenberg, *Marcos and Martial Law in the Philippines* (Ithaca, NY: Cornell University Press, 1979), pp. 262-263.

8. Statement of Benedict J. Kerkvliet, Fellow, Woodrow Wilson Center for International Scholars, Smithsonian Institution; *Political Prisoners in the Philippines*, p. 67.

9. *New York Times*, January 30, 1973, p. 14.

10. The executive secretary was sometimes called "little president" owing to the vast influence of the position. In September 1975 the post was abolished. It was reported that this was done to oust Alejandro Melchor gracefully after a conflict arose between him and Marcos. It was believed that Melchor's close ties with the United States (Melchor graduated from the U.S. Naval Academy in Annapolis) might predispose him to stage a U.S.- instigated military coup.

11. *New York Times*, September 26, 1972, p. 11.

12. Ibid.

13. Ibid., p. 12.

14. Ibid., p. 11.

15. Ibid.

16. Rosenberg, "The End of the Freest Press in the World: Martial Law Comes to the Philippines" (typescript, May 1973), p. 17.

17. *New York Times*, September 26, 1972, p. 11.

18. Ibid.

19. Ibid.

20. Benjamin N. Muego, "The Philippines: From Martial Law to Crisis Government," *Southeast Asian Affairs 1979* (Singapore: Institute of Southeast Asian Studies, 1980), p. 223.

21. Robert O. Tilman, "The Philippines in 1970: A Difficult Decade Begins," *Asian Survey* 9:1 (January 1971): 141.

22. Ibid.

23. Claude A. Buss, *The United States and the Philippines: Background for Policy* (Washington, DC: American Enterprise Institute for Public Policy Research; and Stanford: Hoover Institute on War, Revolution and Peace, 1977), p. 59.

24. For a full discussion of the Malolos government, see Teodoro Agoncillo, *Malolos: The Crisis of the Republic* (Quezon City: University of the Philippines, 1960).

25. *New York Times*, October 4, 1971, p. 1.

26. John H. Adkins, "Philippines 1971: Events of the Year: Trends of the Future," *Asian Survey* 12:1 (January 1970): 82.

27. Mijares, *Conjugal Dictatorship*, pp. 53-54.

28. Ibid.

29. The fact that the ambush of Enrile was staged to provide a reason for the imposition of martial law was confirmed after the February 1986 revolution by Enrile himself. United States Congressional investigators who visited the Philippines in November 1972 speculated about this; they stated that the "attempt to ambush Enrile" as the immediate impetus for martial rule was an afterthought.

30. William Butler, John Humphrey, and G. E. Bisson, *The Decline of Democracy in the Philippines* (Geneva: International Commission of Jurists, 1977), p. 5.

31. Ibid., p. 52.

32. Article VII, 1973 Constitution, in Ferdinand E. Marcos, *The New Philippine Republic: A Third World Approach to Democracy* (Manila: Ministry of Public Information, 1982), pp. 284-287. Hereinafter referred to as the 1973 Constitution.

33. Ibid., Art. VIII, Sec. 2, p. 287.

34. Ibid., Art. IX, Secs. 1 and 3, pp. 291-292.

35. Ibid., Art. IV, pp. 282-284.

36. Ibid., Art. VI, Suffrage, Sec. 1, p. 284.

37. Ibid., Art. XVII, Transitory Provisions, pp. 304-306.

38. Ibid., Art. XVII, Sec. 5, p. 305.

39. Ibid., Art. XVI, Secs. 1 and 2; Art. XVII, Sec. 15, pp. 304-306.

40. Ibid., Art. XVII, Sec. 3, p. 304.

41. Butler, *Decline*, p. 54.

42. Ferdinand E. Marcos, *The Democratic Revolution in the Philippines* (Englewood Cliffs, NJ: Prentice-Hall International, 1979), pp. 184-185.

43. Mijares, *Conjugal Dictatorship*, pp. 451-452; and Butler et al., *Decline*, p. 55.

44. *Javellana v. the Executive Secretary*, quoted in Mijares, *Conjugal Dictatorship*, p. 451.

45. Text of the proclamation in Joaquin G. Bernas, *The 1973 Philippine Constitution: Notes and Cases* (Manila: Rex Book Store, 1974), pp. 14-15.

46. Marcos, *Democratic Revolution*, p. 232.

47. *New York Times*, February 15, 1973, p. 6.

48. Ibid.

49. Ibid., April 1, 1973, p. 13.

50. Ibid., February 15, 1973, p. 6.

51. Ibid., April 1, 1983, p. 13.

52. The following discussion and quotations were based on the Supreme Court decision *Javellana v. Executive Secretary et al.*, L-36142, March 31, 1983, and most specifically to the summary of Chief Justice Roberto Concepcion.

53. Quoted in *New York Times*, April 1, 1973, p. 13.

54. Ibid.

55. Ibid., February 15, 1973, p. 6.

56. Ibid.

57. Marcos, *Democratic Revolution*, p. 188.

58. *New York Times*, April 1, 1973, p. 13.

59. Marcos, *Democratic Revolution*, p. 188.

60. *New York Times*, January 18, 1973, p. 8.

61. Ibid.

62. Larry A. Niksch and Marjorie Niehaus, *The Internal Situation in the Philippines: Current Trends and Future Prospects* (Washington, DC: Congressional Research Service, The Library of Congress, January 20, 1981), p. 10.

63. *New York Times*, August 1, 1983, p. 5.

64. Horacio de la Costa, Jovito R. Salonga, et al., *A Message of Hope to Filipinos Who Care: Containing an Analysis of Three Years of Martial Law, an Evaluation of the New Society . . ."* (Manila, October 1, 1975), p. 20.

65. Butler et al., *Decline*, pp. 62-63. Before the referendum, it was rumored that the Greater Manila area would be converted into a single political unit with Mrs. Imelda Marcos as its head. Several months later petitions were circulated among *barangays* and civic organizations to appoint Mrs. Marcos as the governor of Metro Manila Commission, the integrated government.

66. Lela Garner Noble, "Philippines 1975: Consolidating the Regime," *Asian Survey* 16:2 (February 1976): 179.

67. "Appendix 14, Chronology of Church-State Conflicts in the Philippines . . .," in Rosenberg, *Marcos and Martial Law*, p. 309.

68. *New York Times*, February 2, 1975, p. 12.

69. 62 SCRA G.R. No. L-40004, January 1975; 63 SCRA 275.

70. Letter of Estanislao Fernandez, former associate justice of the Supreme Court, to Congressman Donald M. Frazer, chairperson of the Subcommittee on International Organizations, Committee on International Relations, House of Representatives, United States, July 18, 1975, Human Rights Conditions in Selected Countries and the U.S. Response, p. 500.

71. U.S. Congress, House, Committee on International Relations, *Human Rights in Korea and the Philippines: Implications for U.S. Policy, Hearings before the Subcommittee on International Organizations*, 94th Cong., 1st sess., 1975, Appendix: "The Philippine Situation under Martial Law," prepared by the Solicitor General of the Philippines, June 14, 1975.

72. Noble, "Philippines 1975," p. 179.

73. Jovito R. Salonga, "The Marcos Dictatorship and a Vision of Government" (Unpublished manuscript, Los Angeles, 1984), p. 124.

74. Quoted in ibid.

75. *New York Times*, February 22, 1975, p. 4.

76. *Human Rights in Korea and Philippines*, "Memorandum submitted by Mr. Primitivo Mijares," June 17, 1975, p. 474. Mijares testified in his role as Malacañang Palace insider and wrote the book *The Conjugal Dictatorship of Ferdinand and Imelda Marcos*. He disappeared in 1977. The last thing heard from him was a letter dated January 7, 1977, mailed during his stopover on his way back to Manila. See Vanzi and Poole, *Revolution in the Philippines*, pp. 290-291. Marcos attempted to bribe Mijares to dissuade him from testifying before the U.S. Congress; see Psinakis, *Two Terrorists Meet* (San Francisco: Alchemy Books, 1981), pp. 178-194 (2nd printing); or pp. 186-205 (1st printing).

77. Quoted in ibid., p. 187.

78. "Commission on Elections, Certificates of Canvass of Votes in the National Referendum, Held on February 27 and 28, and Proclamation of the Results Thereof, March 15, 1975," in appendix of *Human Rights in Korea and Philippines*, pp. 414-417.

79. Ibid.

80. 1973 Philippine Constitution, Amendments, pp. 306-307; Butler et al., *Decline*, p. 63.

81. *New York Times*, October 11, 1976, p. 3.

82. Kit G. Machado, "The Philippines in 1977: Beginning a 'Return to Normalcy'?" *Asian Survey* 18:2 (February 1978): 203-204.

83. Ibid.

84. Ibid.

85. Raul P. de Guzman et al., "Citizen Participation and Decision-making under Martial Law . . . " (Manila, December 1974), p. 33. Quoted in David Wurfel, "Martial Law in the Philippines: Methods of Regime Survival," *Pacific Affairs* 50:1 (spring 1977): 10.

86. Machado, "The Philippines 1978: Authoritarian Consolidation Continues," *Asian Survey* 19:2 (February 1979): 132.

87. Ibid.

88. *New York Times*, February 4, 1978, p. 4.

89. Machado, "Philippines 1978," 133.

90. *Far Eastern Economic Review*, April 14, 1978, p. 13.

91. *Peralta et al. v. Comelec et al.* G.R. No. L-47771, 47816, 47767, 47791, and 47827, cited in Muego, "The Philippines," p. 224.

92. Ibid.

93. Carl H. Lande, "Philippine Prospects after Martial Law," *Foreign Affairs* 59 (summer 1981): 1159-1160.

94. Author's notes, April 9, 1978.

95. *Far Eastern Economic Review*, April 9, 1978, p. 13.

96. Ibid.

97. *New York Times*, April 12, 1978, p. 10.

98. Reuben R. Canoy, *The Counterfeit Revolution*: Martial Law in the Philippines (Manila: Philippine Editions Publishing, 1980), p. 178.

99. Ibid., p. 186.

100. Ibid., p. 179.

101. *Far Eastern Economic Review*, April 14, 1978, p. 14.

102. Ibid.

103. Ibid., June 2, 1978.

104. Ibid.

105. Interview with a former Philippine local government official, January 3, 1985.

106. Derek Davies, "Traveller's Tales," *Far Eastern Economic Review*, February 22, 1980.

107. *Far Eastern Economic Review*, February 15, 1980, p. 14.

108. Davies, "Traveller's Tales."

109. *Far Eastern Economic Review*, February 15, 1980, p. 14.

110. Raul P. de Guzman, "The Evolution of Filipino Political Institutions: Prospects for Normalization," *Philippine Journal of Public Administration* 26:3 and 4 (July-October 1982): 210-211.

Chapter 4

A Complete Government Takeover

On January 17, 1981, Marcos announced the termination of martial law, through Proclamation 2045. He also inaugurated the "New Republic," while retaining all martial law decrees, orders, and law-making powers through Amendment Six to the Constitution. He also specifically retained the suspension of the right of the writ of habeas corpus for crimes relating to subversion, insurrection, rebellion, and also conspiracy or proposal to commit such crimes. Marcos could imprison political opponents much as he had under the "New Society" or the martial law regime.

Marcos's action was timed with two significant events: the election of Ronald Reagan as president of the United States and the planned visit of Pope John Paul II to the Philippines in February 1981. By lifting martial law and creating an appearance of normalization, Marcos could strengthen his relationship with the newly elected American administration. He could therefore get unqualified support from an ally because he was more comfortable with President Reagan than with ex-President Carter. The latter's relationship with Marcos was strained by the U.S. human rights policy. The newly elected American president, however, responded warmly to Marcos. Reagan's basic concern with the Philippines was the retention of U.S. military bases to enable America to continue fighting communism and projecting U.S. power in Asia. Before the inauguration of Reagan, Mrs. Marcos met with the president-elect and was reportedly given assurances of more favorable relations. It was also reported that a Reagan aide hinted to the First Lady of the Philippines that "it would be good if Marcos could get a fresh mandate from the people."[1] In deciding to lift martial law, Marcos not only considered the election of Reagan but also sought to minimize papal criticism of his regime, lessening chances of negative publicity and adverse public opinion in the predominantly Catholic Philippines and in the international press.

In February the parliament sitting as a constitutional commission passed proposed amendments to the Constitution. On April 7 a plebiscite was held to approve a shift from a parliamentary to a presidential system of government patterned after the French system. Executive power resided in the president with a prime minister under him. The president was granted the power to name his successor through an executive committee appointed by him to govern the country if he were unable to execute his duties and functions. According to government reports, the amendment was overwhelmingly approved by the voters, including the extension of the presidential term to six years with no limits to reelection. The constitutional amendments also granted to Marcos and his subordinates permanent immunity from being sued in the performance of their official acts and allowed Philippine-born foreigners to buy residential land.

Marcos called a presidential election in June 1981 based on the recent constitutional amendments. As early as April, opposition groups had decided not to participate in the election. They argued that a fair and honest election was not possible under Marcos. Gathering in Baguio City on May 11, they decided to launch a civil disobedience campaign. They agreed to "send teams of activists to various parts of the country to urge people not to vote in the presidential election."[2] An opposition umbrella group, United Democratic Opposition (Unido) demanded that the Commission on Elections be revamped, the voter lists be purged of unqualified and dead people, the campaign be extended to guarantee that the candidates cover the entire Philippines, and Unido be accredited as a minority party. The demands for a free and fair election were not accepted by Marcos;[3] thus, the opposition called for a "total, active, and vigorous" election boycott. Marcos was reportedly dismayed because the absence of a credible opposition candidate could put the legitimacy of the election in question.

Despite the boycott campaign, there was heavy voter turnout because of the threat of prosecution for not participating. The Commission on Elections sent summonses to those who did not participate in the referendum to approve the constitutional amendments.[4] The presidential palace issued a statement declaring that Christians had a moral obligation to vote. Abstention from voting, according to the statement, was a mortal sin. In response, Cardinal Jaime Sin, the archbishop of Manila, issued a pastoral letter proclaiming that the people "were free to exercise their moral judgment whether to vote or not."[5]

Two candidates opposed Marcos in the election. Marcos was suspected of having been instrumental in their participation. He had ordered the Nacionalista Party president, Jose Roy, to "find a candidate after established opposition prospects had decided to boycott the election."[6] Roy had been the leader of the pro-Marcos faction of the president's former political party before he established the KBL. The Nacionalistas chose Alejo Santos to run against Marcos. Santos was a former defense secretary, governor of Bulacan, a province north of Manila, and a Marcos appointee as chairman of the board of the Philippine Veterans Bank. His campaign manager was Francisco Tatad, Marcos's information minister for eleven years.[7] The other candidate was Bartolome Cabangbang of the Federalist Party, which espoused the incorporation of the Philippines as the fifty-first state of the United States. As projected by government sources, Marcos garnered 92% of the votes while Santos and Cabangbang received 5% and 3% respectively.

The following month, Marcos announced the reorganization of his cabinet. Although he reduced the number of ministries to eighteen by merging six ministries into three, he increased his cabinet membership to forty-five by appointing ministers without portfolio. Marcos loyalists were also placed in deputy ministerial positions. He also appointed Cesar Virata, his longtime finance minister as prime minister, and his minister of local government, Jose Roño from Leyte, as his deputy prime minister. Marcos capitalized on Virata's "clean" image and his reputation in international financial circles. Virata lacked a political base, so he did not pose a threat to Marcos. Roño, on the other hand, had gathered support for the president in past elections and referendums.[8] Together with Virata and Roño, several technocrats were appointed or reappointed. Placido Mapa, former chairman of the Development Bank of the Philippines (DBP) was named minister of economic development; Jaime Laya, Central Bank governor; Roberto Ongpin, minister of trade and industry; and Alejandro Melchor, director of DBP and Asian Development Bank (ADB) as presidential adviser.

Marcos continued his firm grip on politics in the Philippines as well as on the full support of the alliance behind his power. He presided over the majority party, the KBL, and its allies in the military and the bureaucracy. His actions were unhampered by the courts and by the fragmented and weak opposition. His relationship with the United States, especially with the Reagan administration, was better than in previous years. In 1982 he was even invited to a state visit in the United States. His last state visit had been in 1966.

In both the United States and the Philippines, Marcos was perceived as the only person capable of governing the country. He was able to lift martial law because the practices established through it had already been institutionalized as integral parts of governance. He was able to rule without the odious connotation of an emergency government or of military rule. Although the system changed in name, the laws that had been put into place for the past nine years of authoritarianism were still in force. The 1981 presidential election and the convening of the Interim *Batasang Pambansa* contributed to the appearance of normalization or a return to an open, participative, and democratic system in spite of the president's continuing power to legislate and to incarcerate anyone indefinitely.

BUREAUCRATIC MARKET EXPANSION

In 1981, it seemed that the Marcos government would remain in office indefinitely, governing through existing policies and procedures and keeping potential opposition groups under control.[9] In a review of the events of 1982, Robert Youngblood concluded:

Again in 1982 Marcos demonstrated his virtuosity as a politician. He kept political opponents divided and at bay, engineered local and regional election victories, soothed Saudi worries about the treatment of Filipino Muslims, and dazzled the Reagan administration during the state visit.[10]

Marcos was at the height of his power in spite of the looming economic crisis. A widespread perception held that there was no alternative to Marcos and that he was therefore preferable to the chaos and unpredictability that would likely follow were he overthrown. Because of Ilocano and Visayan ethnic loyalty to Marcos and his wife, because of the passivity and resignation of the general populace bought by doles of bread and circuses, and because of the benefit and comfort that key elite groups received from the current order, there was no widespread organized opposition to the regime. Marcos's political astuteness and chicanery also helped him to remain in power. The lack of opposition coupled with the the support of an alliance of military personnel, bureaucrats, businesspeople, and regional political leaders enabled Marcos to maintain authoritarian rule. He used legal, constitutional, and economic means, along with reformist ideology, to legitimize his regime. He also used to his advantage a centralized bureaucracy, a strong military, the judiciary, and the media.

Marcos sought to establish internal support by providing his bureaucracy with power over the other sectors of society. To gain such support, Marcos used a system of rewards and punishments directed especially toward national and local politicians, who in turn influenced the mass of others. He centralized and expanded the scope of government, using it as his power base. He used government bureaucracy and its resources in building the alliances for his support. He used the system of patronage or the patron-client network in order to take advantage of government resources, so the scope of government expanded during the Marcos era. Its civilian and military personnel increased. It owned and operated more corporations. The number of government departments and bureaus increased, and their influence became pervasive. The government granted monopolies of key industries and products to selected businesspeople and increased its involvement in the private sector by granting tax exemptions, loan guarantees, and other privileges. It built infrastructure through corrupt contracts; it engaged in deficit spending and consequently incurred more debts in order to sustain its massive operations. Government involvement created greater concentrations of wealth and control of business by a few families, all of whom were related to the Marcoses and their close friends. By the end of the 1970s, most businesses in the Philippines were controlled by eighty-one families with close ties to the Marcos regime. The regime put the entire media at its disposal and curbed the rights of free speech. It established public information and media offices with expanded operations under the offices of both Marcos and his wife.

A large and centralized bureaucracy thus became the base of support for the authoritarian regime. When the umbrella political party, the (KBL), was established, it consisted of all incumbent government officials, cabinet members, provincial governors, and town and city mayors. It also included members of the military as well as business cronies of the president. The political party became the ruling party, with no ideology except that of its loyalty to Marcos.

ESTABLISHING INTERNAL SUPPORT

The centerpiece of Marcos's rule was the centralized and expanded civilian and military bureaucracies—the locus of politics and the center of the political activities of the regime. After imposing martial law, Marcos issued General Order No. 1 on

September 21, 1972, which placed under him the entire operation of the Philippine government. The order stated:

By virtue of the powers vested in me by the Constitution as Commander-in-Chief of the Armed Forces of the Philippines, [I] do hereby proclaim that I shall govern the nation and direct the operation of the entire Government, including all its agencies and instrumentalities, in my capacity and shall exercise all the powers and prerogatives appurtenant and incident to my position as Commander-in-Chief of all the armed forces of the Philippines.[11]

Immediately thereafter, Marcos also promulgated the reorganization of the government as his first presidential decree. On September 24, 1972, he enacted the Integrated Reorganization Plan, which had resulted from a study by the Commission on Reorganization, a joint executive-legislative group. The reorganization's desired objectives were "promoting simplicity, economy and efficiency in the government to enable it to pursue programs consistent with national goals for accelerated social and economic development; and improving the service for transacting public business in government agencies."[12] In fact, the result of that plan was to ensure that nothing interfered with the exercise of power by the military or the bureaucracy.

Marcos ensured the loyalty of the bureaucracies, both military and civilian, by expanding their influence and power. He accomplished the expansion in two ways. He first used law and terror to limit the powers of other societal groups and institutions. He next granted perks and resources to bureaucrats.

THE MILITARY

The military was a critical bureaucratic branch during martial law, and Marcos spared no effort to ensure that the military was strong and supportive of his authoritarian ambitions. Marcos increased his ability to control the armed forces, elevated its status, and involved it in traditionally nonmilitary or civilian activities.

To increase the military's prominent position and priority in government, during his first term Marcos appointed himself secretary of national defense.[13] He began the implementation of the socioeconomic military program created in 1958. Marcos envisioned the military playing an important role in his economic program. In his first State of the Nation Address, he called for (1) increasing training, (2) supplying new equipment, (3) heightening morale, (4) reforming the nation's police forces, (5) activating a Philippine coast guard, and (6) expanding the military's socioeconomic development program.[14]

The Marcos administration's Four-Year Economic Program stated that the military's personnel, resources, and organization could be used for economic as well as for military ends in order to maximize the use of resources.

To enhance the education of military officers, the National Defense College, which was established in 1963, started regularly offering courses in 1966.[15] Under the heading of civic action, the army became involved in an array of activities previously performed by the national and local police agencies, such as the guarding and monitoring of local and national elections.

Civic action programs such as those in engineering and health were designed to win the sympathy and support of the populace. Those programs were also called ideological-support activities for counterinsurgency operations, especially in rural areas where there were incidents of dissent and antigovernment activities. The U.S. Army Special Forces, known as the Green Berets, participated in civic action activities with Filipino soldiers in areas such as Samar, Albay, Palawan, Nueva Ecija, and Nueva Vizcaya, provinces with histories of insurgency or with a potential for it. The Green Berets came from a U.S. post in Okinawa to work "on a co-equal integrated basis with the Armed Forces of the Philippines counterpart [civic action] team" for four years in some twelve provinces.[16]

The military became more aware of its potential role in politics because of its expanded role. New possibilities opened for involving the military in developmental activities. Those activities were not only carried out through Marcos's initiative but also aided by the United States in exchange for Marcos's support of the U.S. venture in Southeast Asia, the Vietnam War.

Between 1965 and 1972, Marcos was able to expand the role of the military through increased resources from the United States. In exchange for Philippine support of the United States in Vietnam, Marcos changed his position on involving the Philippine troops in Vietnam. As Senate president, he objected to any Philippine participation, but when he became president of the country, he vigorously campaigned for the approval of the Philippine Congress to send the Philippine Civic Action Group (Philcag) to Vietnam.

Before Marcos's time, the military was not a significant branch of the bureaucracy. Its resources were limited because there existed no external or internal threats to the established government of the country. The civilian bureaucracy was also able to perform the day-to-day functions of government. Local police troops under city and municipal governments and the PC, the national police, were able to deal with law enforcement in the country.

It was only during the presidency of Ramon Magsaysay, in its campaign against the Huk rebels, that the military enjoyed a prominent role in national government. Magsaysay, a charismatic and populist politician, was the former secretary of national defense, whose success in the antiinsurgency campaign made him popular. His success could be attributed to a combination of military and nonmilitary means, such as offering land, increased services, and resettlement to Huks who surrendered. After the government suppressed the Huks, the military continued in its unassuming role. Not until the presidency of Marcos did the department of national defense once again became prominent.

Under martial law, the military continued to expand in membership and resources. There were various estimates of its growth. The military increased from 56,000 to 58,000 in 1972, to about from 223,000 to 236,000 in 1982. Its 1972 budget was $82 million; its 1982 budget, $1 billion.[17] In 1980 the military budget accounted for 12.4% of government expenditures. Between 1976 and 1977, its share rose to 19%. From 1971 the budget grew 300%, after factoring in inflation, to 800% in current prices.[18] In 1983, 35% was allocated to the military.[19]

Marcos expanded the mission and centralized the organization of the armed forces. As the commander-in-chief, he directly supervised and controlled the armed forces. Directly under the president was the minister of national defense, Ponce-Enrile, who was also named martial law administrator. Divided into several regional commands, the country was directly under the operational command of the chief of staff. Since 1972 the chief of staff's power had also grown considerably along with his power to bypass the commands of the various services: the army, the navy, the air force, the PC and Integrated National Police (INP), the Integrated Civilian Home Defense Force, the Presidential Security Command (PSC), and the various intelligence and counterinsurgency networks.[20]

Marcos considered the military a partner of the civilian bureaucracy with a threefold role: "(1) assistance in the implementation of development goals, (2) direct participation in development programs, and (3) creation of an atmosphere conducive to national development."[21] His reliance on the military as well as on his mandate to expand its role boosted its prestige and image. The military gratefully received Marcos's gesture of confidence. Its position in the Philippine bureaucracy had never been accorded such importance as during the Marcos era.

The military, in turn, became the dispenser of patronage, to some extent replacing local politicians and members of Congress. Local police forces were also indulged in the INP and PC, so those in need of help did not have to go through local officials but could seek direct access to AFP officers. The increasing importance of the military was observed by Harold W. Maynard when he interviewed senior armed forces officers. According to Maynard:

Ordinary civilians, as well as families of military men, now regularly call upon senior officers to plead assistance in getting jobs, solving family problems, processing applications, securing community development projects, or replacing inept local officials. . . . Scenes which used to take place in the offices of Senators and Congressmen are increasingly taking place in the offices of generals and colonels. Traditional patron-client relationships have simply moved to a new arena under martial law.[22]

Military attaches were assigned to Philippine missions and embassies abroad. Promotions, high salaries, and other fringe benefits were given to the members of the armed forces. Training programs and courses were given to the ranks in public administration, management, and national security studies. Defense was allocated the highest percentage of the national budget, replacing the allocation for health, social services, and education. High-ranking generals were retained though they reached retirement age because of their assured loyalty to the president. Those who were retired were given key positions in the civilian bureaucracy or were welcomed by public and private corporations. The military became a more visible instrument of bureaucracy and national policy under the sole control of Marcos. Marcos characterized the military variously as a "catalyst of social change," a "training institution for national leaders," the "defender of the seat of government," a "nation builder," and a "model of national discipline and self-reliance."[23]

The military also exercised judicial functions. Marcos issued General Order No. 8 (1972), creating military courts to try cases of subversion, insurrection, and other crimes against the state or cases involving national security. Some prisoners were charged with both criminal offenses and political offenses to assure their prosecution. The right of the writ of habeas corpus was rescinded so that the military could prolong the detention of suspected subversives—usually Marcos opponents. The civilian courts also had limited jurisdiction, or in most cases no jurisdiction, over cases brought by the military. The president or the chief of staff of the armed forces could also transfer cases from the civilian court to the autonomous military courts. All the military tribunals, which were composed of five-member commissions or single-member provost courts, were under the Judge Advocate General Office (JAGO) of the AFP. The JAGO also exercised prosecutorial and investigatory functions. It operated autonomously and had its own rules of procedures.[24]

After martial law was lifted in 1981 and the wide jurisdiction of military courts was limited, military prosecutors tried to secure permission from the Ministry of Justice to prosecute "civilian" trials involving national security. The military courts also continued to try cases brought to it before martial law was lifted. They investigated cases and pressured civilian judges, as well as their lawyers, by threatening the loss of business and intimidating witnesses so that they would not appear at trials or hearings. Human rights lawyers defending the accused were threatened with the Presidential Commitment Order, which would hold them in indefinite detention unless their release was authorized by the president. In 1982 ten members of a human rights lawyers group called Free Legal Assistance Group (FLAG) were threatened with the Presidential Commitment Order; in addition, deliberate delays plagued the conclusion of cases.[25]

According to the Lawyers Committee for International Human Rights:

The most common complaint of defense lawyers handling national security cases is that trials are protracted once they start, and long periods often elapse before they are even begun. Although a combination of factors appears to account for such delays, they appear to be partially due to deliberate efforts by the military to string out cases in which there is not enough evidence to support conviction. We were told of numerous cases in which hearings were scheduled but had to be adjourned several times because the military prosecutors or witnesses failed to show. As a result of these and other delays, few national security cases have been completed on the merits since martial law was imposed, though thousands have been arrested on national security grounds.[26]

Marcos was effective in preventing either the Congress or the courts from providing any check to the activity of the military, so he alone had sole control, but he depended on the military to implement martial law, and the military's increased power made it susceptible to corruption and arbitrary abuses of authority. In its fight against subversion, the armed forces violated human rights. It engaged in indiscriminate acts of violence against civilians. In 1974, there were 1,000 to 2,000 people were killed when the army staged a massive attack on the city of Jolo without sparing civilian targets. The government used bombs, napalm, and heavy artillery.[27]

Disappearances and extra-judicial executions, in the Philippines known as "salvaging," became more common after 1981. Salvaging occurred when someone arrested by the military was claimed to have disappeared and then later found killed.[28] The military used torture and force in investigating suspects. Cases of human rights violations by the military were reported throughout the Marcos years.The Task Force Detainees affiliated with the Association of Major Religious Superiors, the International Commission of Jurists, and Amnesty International, as well as other human rights groups, has documented various human rights abuses committed by the Marcos government and mainly perpetrated by the armed forces and paramilitary groups. The following were the most prevalent cases documented and investigated by Philippine and international groups:

1. Persistent . . . extralegal practices by government agents, which, in addition to torture, include the "disappearance" and extra-judicial executions of real or perceived opponents of government; the absence, or inadequacy, of investigation when complaints of such human rights violations are made;

2. arbitrary arrest and detention, including largely short-term detention of persons for the non-violent exercise of their human rights and the use of torture;

3. the detention of political prisoners without trial within a reasonable time, or trial according to procedures in violation of recognized norms.[29]

The military also engaged in "search-and-destroy" operations wherein soldiers shot first before they investigated and then automatically accused anyone killed as a member of the NPA, the Communist insurgent group.[30] The accusations legitimized the "search-and-destroy" missions without ascertaining the identity of the enemy.

According to Frederick Brown and Carl Ford in their report to the Committee on Foreign Relations of the U.S. Senate in September 1984:

A number of people in northeastern Luzon mentioned to us one particular operation in June in which they feared artillery and air-delivered bombs had been employed indiscriminately. They suspected that many civilians had been killed. In response to our queries, officials stated that aircraft had not been used in the operation. Later, one military source privately contradicted these assurances and stated emphatically that the AFP had used aircraft to bomb suspected NPA concentrations. This report was later confirmed beyond reasonable doubt.[31]

The armed forces used "strategic hamletting" or "clustering" to isolate rural villages from the NPA. They moved and resettled inhabitants of entire villages to remove them as potential bases of guerrilla support. The threat of harassment, arrest, detention, torture, and extrajudicial execution discouraged vocal and organized opposition to the Marcos regime. The threat posed by Marcos's military, with its monopoly of force, disorganized and weakened opposition against Marcos.

The influence of the military in Philippine life increased. Before 1972 the armed forces exercised little influence and civilian authorities had a greater degree of control over them. According to Carolina Hernandez in her study on the extent of civilian control of the military, after 1972 the military's influence was increased, whereas the degree of civilian control decreased.[32] Cardinal Jaime Sin, the archbishop of Manila, observed that

Daily we experience the increasing militarization of our lives: the pervasive surveillance of citizens who express dissent democratically by military intelligence; the lack of mercy and prudence shown by special military units against suspected criminals; the use of torture to extract information; the unexpected wealth of many military officers.[33]

THE JUDICIARY AND THE COURTS

As he expanded the role of the military, Marcos limited the power of the judiciary. To ensure that his policies were implemented as he saw necessary, Marcos needed to curb the independence and review powers of the Supreme Court. Directly or indirectly, Marcos exerted pressure on the Supreme Court to give him a free rein; in turn, the court exercised a great deal of self-regulation to avoid confrontation with Marcos.

That self-regulation can be seen in the court's handling of cases challenging the suspension of the writ of habeas corpus. A petition before the Supreme Court questioned the justification for the suspension. The decision in *Lansang v. Garcia*, handed down on December 11, 1971, limited judicial inquiry into the question of whether the executive abused discretion or acted arbitrarily in the suspension of the writ. It did not express any opinion on the correctness of the president's action, nor did it examine the facts that resulted from the suspension. The decision stated that "the Court was not prepared to hold that the executive had acted arbitrarily or [had] gravely abused his discretion when he then concluded that public safety and national security required the suspension of the writ of habeas corpus."[34] Regarding the court's competence, the decision declared its function to be "is merely to check, not to supplant the executive, or to ascertain merely whether he has gone beyond the constitutional limits of his jurisdiction, not to exercise the power vested in him or to determine the wisdom of his act."[35]

After Marcos imposed the 1973 Constitution, the Supreme Court received petitions to prevent executives from collecting, certifying, and reporting the results of the consultation of the Citizens' Assemblies used to legitimize the Constitution. A divided court declared that "whether or not the plebiscite or referendum could validly be held and should be restrained" was moot. In deciding the *Ratification Cases* through *Javellana v. the Executive Secretary*, the Supreme Court paved the way for the constitutional justification of the legitimacy of Marcos's authoritarian regime.

The ratification of the 1973 Constitution strengthened the presidency. Once again, the justices of the Supreme Court took the oath of office to signify their acquiescence to the new Constitution. Under the 1973 Constitution, appointment of justices did not require legislative review. Appointments to the Supreme court were not subject to confirmation or consent by an independent body such as the

Commission on Appointments in Congress. The president had the sole power to appoint justices to appellate courts and judges to the Supreme Court. The number of Supreme Court justices was increased from eleven to fifteen in the 1973 Constitution, allowing Marcos to pack the Supreme Court with judges whose loyalty to him was assured.

A provision of the 1973 Constitution could also be interpreted as restrictive to the jurisdiction of the Supreme Court. Article X, Section 5(a) of the 1973 Constitution provided that "the Supreme Court shall have jurisdiction over all cases in which only an error or question of law is involved."[36] The provision that required a majority of ten affirmative votes to declare a treaty, executive agreement, or law unconstitutional was another aspect of the law that presumed the constitutionality of executive acts.

Marcos declared that the Constitution was ratified, although a plebiscite, as required by the 1935 charter, was not held. The legality of the ratification was questioned, but the Supreme Court declared that no more judicial obstacles prevented its enforcement, thereby avoiding having to decide the legality of the document. In support of Marcos, the court did not present any judicial hindrance that might have put the ratification to question.

Under the transitory provisions, the president increased his authority over appointing or dismissing judges. According to Section 10, all judges would continue in office unless replaced or otherwise retained by Marcos through a presidential decree. Throughout the years of martial law, judges had uncertain tenure because they were under the constant threat of losing their positions if their behavior did not conform to presidential will.

The court, whose membership by this time was mostly composed of Marcos appointees, was willing to give Marcos free rein in declaring the acts of his opponents as acts of rebellion. In the case *Lansang v. Garcia*, the Supreme Court noted the existence of rebellion and cited the existence of the NPA as proof of the existence of rebellion. Although acknowledging the existence of rebellion, the Supreme Court did not enquire into the magnitude or extent that rebellion. The reality of the threat posed by the rebellion should have been measured and evaluated by the presidential proclamation. The Supreme Court accepted the mere existence of the NPA as a threat; thus, the Supreme Court was, in a way, privy to the imposition of martial law. Future Supreme Court decisions would favor and justify the actions of the president. In fine legalese, the court would avoid making clear decisions. It left Marcos's acts as faits accomplis and placed them under the rubric of politics—and thus beyond the scope of judicial inquiry. As the justices carried out their duties and fulfilled their responsibilities, they could not discount the threat of violence and assassination if they failed to toe the line.

In 1983 Marcos constituted the "Integrity Council," chaired by the minister of justice to screen candidates for judges and to recommend those who were fit to be appointed. The council commented that only half of the current 1,600 judges were qualified and fit for office; however, most of them were later reappointed by the president. The enactment of the Judiciary Reform Act of 1983 also paved the way for the abolition of all existing courts lower than the Supreme Court, except the

Sandiganbayan and the Court of Tax Appeals. The act was formulated by the Presidential Committee on Judicial Reorganization appointed by Marcos. The committee was composed of two Supreme Court justices and the deputy minister of justice with the chief justice of the Supreme Court as co-chairman with the minister of justice. The formation of a presidential commission with Supreme Court justices appointed to it put the highest court in a position inferior to that of the president.

As an expression of Marcos's authority and of the institution of a new order, the act replaced the courts in name but not necessarily in their functions. The Court of Appeals, which was the appellate court directly below the Supreme Court, was renamed the Intermediate Appellate Court. The membership of the intermediate court was increased from forty-five to fifty. The purpose of the intermediate court was "to hear appeal cases not expressly reserved for the Supreme Court and [the court] was given additional jurisdiction over certain cases involving questions of fact."[37]   Regional trial courts replaced courts of first instance, circuit criminal courts, and agrarian relations courts.[38] The municipal courts remained on the lowest rung of the judicial ladder.

Marcos's actions weakened the Supreme Court and the entire judiciary. As discussed above, even the military influenced the courts and its proceedings; for example, the military gave briefings to justices who heard cases relating to national security. At certain points, the judiciary even abdicated its authority by inaction. In *Garcia Padilla v. Ponce-Enrile*, the Supreme Court abdicated its authority to review the president's power to make decrees in matters of national security. The court declared "that when the President takes action to respond to a 'grave emergency,' whose existence he alone can affirm, the judiciary can, with becoming modesty, ill afford to assume authority to check or reverse or supplant the presidential actions."[39]

During the martial law years, the Supreme Court provided an image of legitimacy and continuity to the regime while it was increasingly being subordinated to presidential authority. Its jurisdiction and independence contracted while the scope of authoritarian influence and control expanded. To survive, the judiciary bent to presidential authority as did other government branches. In the process, it institutionalized the authoritarian regime.

DISBANDED CONGRESS

Although limiting the power of the judiciary was key to Marcos's plans, also important was limiting the influence of other political and social institutions. By imposing martial law, Marcos was able to eliminate all sources of resistance; for example, Congress was an early target of Marcos's grab for power. Senators Eva Estrada Kalaw, Ramon Mitra, Ambrosio Padilla, Gerardo Roxas, and Jovito Salonga petitioned the Supreme Court to prohibit Marcos "from interfering with the performance of their lawful duties as senators of the Philippines."[40] Senators tried to enter the halls of Congress on January 22, the opening date of the legislature as set forth in the 1935 Constitution; however, they were unable to do so because the doors were padlocked and guarded by soldiers.

In *Roxas v. Melchor* (Alejandro Melchor was the executive secretary of the Marcos cabinet), the petitioner, Roxas, sought to compel by mandamus the president and president pro tempore of the Senate to call the Senate into session in accordance with the 1935 Constitution, which provided for the calling of Congress into session on the fourth Monday of January every year.[41] The petition was denied by the then impotent Supreme Court.

THE OPPOSITION

In his efforts to consolidate his power, Marcos did not avoid directly repressing opponents when necessary. Marcos jailed political leaders and opponents on the pretext that they were planning to assassinate him and to overthrow the government he had established. After martial law was imposed, some politicians fled to the United States; others less fortunate were placed under house arrest.

Opposition parties could not challenge Marcos in the courts, so their activities were confined to writing manifestos, circulating articles, and speaking in small groups. Marcos clamped down on these activities by making "rumor mongering" punishable. With the regime's takeover of the national newspapers, radio, and television stations, both the voices and the participants of opposition media greatly decreased. Relatively open dissent was heard only in the churches and universities.

For their political survival, local officials accepted Marcos's authoritarian takeover as a fait accompli. Because the regime monopolized patronage, they needed to be allied with Marcos to continue occupying their positions as well as to be able to continue gathering favors for their constituents. The majority of the people and their political leaders felt threatened by the regime, so they did not openly object as Marcos centralized the government and legitimized his authority. The repression of legitimate means of dissent, however, led to the growth of underground opposition. The Muslim rebels, along with the Communist Party and its armed wing, the NPA, increased their activities and gained more supporters and sympathizers. They continued their work as far as possible without the regime knowing of their activities. Dissatisfaction with the regime won them sympathy and support. They won over those who felt that armed opposition was the only avenue left for throwing out the Marcos regime and instituting reform in Philippine society.

Fighting Muslim rebels in Mindanao cost Marcos heavily in both money and soldiers. The costs and the threat of sanctions from Arab oil-producing countries, who supported the Muslims in the southern Philippines, forced the Marcos regime to negotiate with the Moro National Liberation Front in Tripoli, Libya, under the auspices of nations selected by the Organization of the Islamic Conference. The Tripoli Agreement called for a ceasefire and for the establishment of an autonomous government for Mindanao within the territory and sovereignty of the Republic of the Philippines. Despite the supposed autonomy of that Mindanao government, however, Marcos was able to keep it under the direct control of the central government because the Muslims, divided into different factions, were disunited in their struggle against Marcos. Marcos co-opted some Muslim leaders, but others forged links with the NPA. The Muslim rebellion continued to be more than a distraction for the Marcos government.

Marcos's control of the various political forces and the disunity and weakness of the above-ground opposition contributed to the institutionalization of the authoritarian regime. While the opposition groped for strategy, unity, ideology, and leadership, Marcos presided over and built an alliance of supporters to his regime. At the same time, despite an increase in the forces for violent opposition, Marcos was able to keep them sufficiently off-balance to maintain his power.

CIVILIAN BUREAUCRACY AND LOCAL GOVERNMENT

Critical to his limiting the power of other institutions was Marcos's ability to expand the civilian bureaucracy and to ensure the support of key bureaucrats. He ensured their support by increasing the power of the bureaucracy in the name of professionalism and technical efficiency. In fact, his rhetoric even supported cutting down the size of the bureaucracy in the name of efficiency. After he imposed martial law, Marcos promulgated the reorganization of government as his first presidential decree. On September 24, 1972, he enacted the Integrated Reorganization Plan (IRP), which resulted from a study by the Commission on Reorganization, a joint executive-legislative group. The objectives of the reorganization were "promoting simplicity, economy and efficiency in the government to enable it to pursue programs consistent with national goals for accelerated social and economic development; and improving the service for transacting public business in government agencies."[42]

That first decree was meant to set the tone for reform. The IRP reduced the number of government departments; however, just after its enactment, more government departments—later to be called ministries—proliferated, and new offices, which were not in the plan, were created. Thus, "the IRP ceased to be integrated even in its first year of implementation."[43] Some civil servants called the plan "RIP" (Rest in Peace). Changes in the original plan, made because of political considerations, resulted in a very different governmental structure. Departments and governmental offices proliferated. Some duplicated the function of others but had to be retained. New offices were also created to employ more people and perform functions taken over by government; for example, the Ministry of Human Settlements, headed by Mrs. Marcos, was referred to as the umbrella ministry because it performed multifarious functions that included duties of other departments. It intruded on the ministries of local government, community development, education, and other areas, depending on Mrs. Marcos's whims and discretion.

In addition to reorganization, regionalization and decentralization were envisioned by the IRP to improve government efficiency and effectiveness. The authoritarian structure, however, promoted the opposite: centralization, the concentration of power and decision making. The ministries' main functions and control continued to be concentrated in the capital. Policy decisions were still made in Manila. After more than a decade, the regionalization scheme was still not operational because political authority had not been disbursed during the Marcos years. According to Ledivina Cariño, "Local governments tend to be mere extensions of the central government except where a local official [was] strong enough, or his territory rich enough, to take up the task of running his own programs."[44]

With the regionalization scheme, the country's provinces were organized into twelve regions, with Metro Manila as the thirteenth region or the National Capital region. Development planning and implementation were supposed to be done in integrated areas or regional units to assure autonomy and decentralization. Regions IX and XII were designated autonomous regions. Those regions included the predominantly Muslim provinces of Lanao, Maguindanao, Cotabato, Sultan Kudarat, Basilan, Sulu, Tawi-tawi, and Zamboanga. Structures were created to plan and administer those regions; in addition, Letter of Instruction No. 22 created Regional Development Councils to work at the regional level and to coordinate with the national planning body, the National Economic Development Authority (NEDA).[45]

To coordinate and monitor the development efforts, the president created ad hoc offices and appointed several influential persons in each region. Those offices included, at one time or another, Presidential Regional Officers for Development (PRODs), Presidential Action Officers (PRAOs), Coordinating Officers for Program Execution (COPE), and the Presidential Regional Monitoring Officers (PREMO). In assessing the conduct of those officers, it was found that they "did not effectively deliver their duties and responsibilities . . . [and] if ever they [did], they acted as persons in the 'hierarchy of power.'"[46] According to a study written in 1983, only two PREMOs had been appointed: the First Lady for the National Capital Region and one of her relatives for the Visayan region.[47] All the officials were presidential appointees. Marcos usually appointed powerful local persons also loyal to him. Their closeness to Marcos assured them of direct communication and speedy responses from the government, as well as access to resources and funds, all of which, in turn, assured the president's control over them.

Marcos relied on the most influential persons and politicians in each region, and later on local military leaders, to look after his interests. By 1978 six out of twelve regions had military PRODs: Col. Gil Manuel in Region 2, Colonel Benjamin Santos in Region 2, Brig. Gen. Mario Espina in Region 6, Admiral Romulo Espaldon in Region 9, Brig. Gen. Alfonso Alcoseba in Region 10, and Col. Emilio Ahorro in Region 11.[48]

Marcos connected himself to the grass roots through recognized local and regional leaders; for example, Marcos had his defense minister, Juan Ponce-Enrile, as the influential leader of Cagayan Valley (Region 2), the Romualdezes in Leyte, Ramon Durano in Cebu, and Ali Dimaporo in Lanao. All local officials, after 1973, served at the pleasure of the president. He appointed individuals recommended by the regional leaders. All local officials therefore owed their positions to the president. Their appointments to government positions were highly regarded as favors and did not necessarily result from their qualifications. Those who were favored owed gratitude and returned the favors to the person responsible for the appointments. The government easily mobilized local leaders in getting followers to vote favorably for Marcos in the referendums and in distributing pork-barrel funds to local constituents before elections.

In Autonomous Regions 9 and 12, Marcos appointed the Regional Executive Council, which acted as the regional manager, and the Sangguiniang Pampook, which acted as the legislative body. In Metro Manila, an area comprised of four major cities and thirteen municipalities, the president created the Metro Manila Commission, which had legislative as well as administrative powers. Marcos appointed his wife governor of Metro Manila, and the commission was placed directly under the president. All government services were integrated under the commission. Polices forces were unified under the command of the INP and PC. Again, because of the organization, the president controlled the regions, reinforcing the centralized tendencies of the authoritarian government.[49]

In 1975 arbitrary dismissals weeded out the "notoriously undesirable persons" from government service. A study of the College of Public Administration, University of the Philippines, found that no clear guidelines served as a basis for those dismissals. The dismissal list even included those who had long since died, retired, or left their offices. Individuals with strong "connections" were able to escape dismissals. As in other programs, the enthusiasm for personnel improvement waned, so much so that in 1981 Marcos expressed once more his dismay at government corruption and asked that further studies be conducted to assess its nature and causes.[50] Corruption, however, became more difficult to combat, especially when real reform of the system would mean disenfranchising the newly entrenched elites created by the New Society.

By providing opportunities for corrupt aggrandizement and by increasing the scope of the bureaucrats' domain, Marcos was able to ensure for himself the support of the bureaucracy and thus, to a great degree, his power in society.

BUREAUCRATIC OWNERSHIP OF BUSINESS

An integral component of Marcos's expansion of the bureaucracy was giving the government direct control over business operations. That control was essential for meeting the demands of oligarchic power groups. It also had the effect of giving Marcos more resources to satisfy the demands of burearcracies for power and money. The number of government departments and bureaus increased. Their influence and concern became pervasive. The government granted monopolies to key industries and products to selected businesspeople, and the government increased its involvement in the private sector by granting tax exemptions, loan guarantees, and other privileges. It engaged in deficit spending and consequently incurred more debt in order to sustain its massive operations. To manipulate the media, the government established publicity and information offices with expanded operations under the control of Marcos and his wife.

With the increased government activity and expansion of the public sphere came the establishment of public enterprise. Public enterprise, or government-owned or controlled corporations, dramatically increased in number and size during the Marcos years. In fewer than ten years after martial law, the number of government-owned corporations increased from thirty-two to ninety-three. Sixty-two of them were created by presidential decrees or executive orders. Only one public enterprise was created by an act of the parliament. From the Commonwealth era to 1972, only thirty-two corporations were created, and they were all established through the legislature. An extensive amount of public money was poured into those corporations.[51] From 1979 to 1982, "the national government spent an average of 7.6 billion pesos for subsidies and equities and seven billion for capital investments, or a total average of 15 billion pesos annually."[52] According to Philippine Central Bank reports, 72.9% of the total public debt was incurred by government corporations, leaving the national government with the remaining 27.1%. According to a Commission on Audit (COA) reports in 1982, "assets of public enterprises totalled 379.6 billion, as against 167.6 billion and 10.8 billion of national government and local government."[53]

The dramatic increase in the number of public corporations and the resources that those corporations controlled resulted from several government takeovers of so-called oligarch companies, meaning businesses owned by Marcos's opponents. During his reign, Marcos also ordered government takeovers of various businesses of his "cronies" to bail them out of bankruptcy. These takeovers were justified as vital to national interest. The government increased its capitalization of ailing businesses to assure their survival. It also assumed and guaranteed all loans to such businesses. Often, they had already become unprofitable, so government takeover simply meant the absorption of their losses.

According to Budget Minister Manuel S. Alba, those ailing businesses had become so weak that 30% to 32% of the total cash requirements for the public enterprises came from the government. In spite of the drain they put on the government budget, these public enterprises produced little. A World Bank report stated that their contribution to gross domestic product (GDP) was only 3%.[54]

Public enterprises claimed exemptions from national government regulations on hiring, pay, and personnel policies. These exemptions from civil service regulations and the great discretionary power of unaccountable authority led to irresponsible operations.

The expansion of public enterprise thus contributed to the increase in public borrowing, in the scope of authoritarian control, and in the opportunity to use government resources to win support. Because of increased government involvement in economic activities, the public sphere grew. With the growth in governmental responsibilities came a growth in the national financial burden as well.

Government ministers were often given direct control of business. Defense Minister Juan Ponce-Enrile took over a conglomerate of fourteen companies owned by the Jacintos because doing so was in the national interest and because the companies had "outstanding obligations to government." The companies included Jacinto Steel, Jacinto Iron and Iron Sheets, Ferro Products, Beatriz Marketing, J&P Shipping Corporation, publishing companies, a newspaper, and two radio stations. The minister put those companies under the charge of Armed Forces Chief of Staff General Romeo Espino, who in turn placed army officials in executive positions. The regime also took over the Manila Electric Company (Meralco) and the Lopez media conglomerate of one daily newspaper, six television stations, and twenty-two radio stations. The facilities of the *Manila Chronicle* were taken over by Benjamin Romualdez, brother of Mrs. Marcos, for publishing the *Times-Journal*.

Marcos cronies Eduardo Cojuangco and Ponce-Enrile were the only two civilians in the Group of Twelve who planned martial law. Cojuangco administered the Coconut Federation (Cocofed), an organization that controlled the industry. All farmers were required by government to participate in Cocofed. When the price of coconut oil was high, the government imposed a levy toward a fund to stabilize the production and price of coconut. The original idea for the establishing the fund was to tax farmers in order to subsidize domestic coconut cooking oil prices.[55]

When the price of coconut fell, the coconut tax was used to fund scholarships, insurance, and other benefits for planters and farmers. It later turned out that the contributors were not qualified to receive benefits from the fund. The money was used mainly to purchase the United Coconut Planters Bank (UCPB) and the United Coconut Mills, Inc. (Unicom). The former was the First United Bank, originally owned by the Cojuangco family. The latter was the company that controlled 85% of the coconut milling industry through presidential decrees and government subsidies. Those organizations were not subject to government auditing in spite of their use of public funds. Farmers owned 70% of the bank, but holders of the remaining 30% controlled the bank.

The president of the Philippine National Bank, Roberto Benedicto, a college fraternity brother of Marcos, was given control of the sugar industry. Sugar is one of the most important cash crops in the Philippines. Marcos ordered that all disposition of sugar needed his approval. He created the Philippine Exchange Company (Philex) and later the National Sugar Trading (Nasutra), under Benedicto's control, to take charge of all sugar trading; as a result, farmers could not take their sugar to a mill of their choice. They instead got receipts from the government for their sugar. The government then sold the receipts to competitive sugar brokers. When the sugar was sold, the farmers waited for government payments, the amounts of which were decided solely by the government. Even when the world price for sugar was forty-six cents a pound, the price of Philippine sugar was fixed at twelve cents; thus, the sugar producers did not enjoy the sugar boom in 1974. According to a study by the University of the Philippines School of Economics, the sugar monopoly resulted in the loss of between 11.6 billion to 14.4 billion pesos to sugar producers and in increased prices with no corresponding increase in foreign exchange or in the efficiency of operations.[56]

Despite the decline in demand and the resulting slump in the sugar market, the Marcos regime increased milling capacity and operations. It approved the financing of new sugar mills at $40 million each. It was reported that the decision to finance the mills was triggered by the kickback payment that might accrue from the financing. The Marubeni Corporation (Japan) paid 12%, or about $6 million, to Benedicto for each sugar mill it equipped.[57]

To increase the status and power of the government, Marcos increased its control of the economy. His rhetoric to the contrary, the effect of Marcos's nationalization of industry was the enrichment of his friends rather than the efficient and fair use and distribution of resources.

NOTES

1. *Far Eastern Economic Review*, January 2, 1981, p. 26.

2. *New York Times*, May 12, 1981, p. 4.

3. *Far Eastern Economic Review*, May 1, 1981, p. 16.

4. Ibid., June 19, 1981, p. 13.

5. Ibid.

6. Ibid., July 31, 1981, pp. 8-9.

7. Ibid., June 5, 1981, p. 32.

8. Ibid., July 31, 1981, p. 8.

9. Larry A. Niksch and Marjorie Niehaus, *The Internal Situation in the Philippines: Current Trends and Future Prospects* (Washington, D.C.: Congressional Research Service, Library of Congress, January 20, 1981), p. 1.

10. Robert Youngblood, "The Philippines in 1982: Marcos Gets Tough with Domestic Critics," *Asian Survey* 23:2 (February 1983): 215.

11. "General Order No. 1, That President Ferdinand E. Marcos Will Govern the Nation and Direct the Operation of the Entire Government," in David A. Rosenberg, *Marcos and Martial Law in the Philippines* (Ithaca, NY: Cornell University Press, 1979), p. 241.

12. Presidential Commission on Reorganization, *Organizing for Development* (presentation prepared for the Interim Batasang Pambansa, June 13, 1978, Manila), quoted in Victoria A. Bautista, "Structure of the Philippine Administrative System" (Manila: niversity of the Philippines, College of Public Administration, 1985, typescript).

13. Primitivo Mijares, *The Conjugal Dictatorship of Ferdinand and Imelda Marcos I* (San Francisco: Union Square Publications, 1976), p. 130; and *New York Times*, December 29, 1965, pp. 3 and 5.

14. Quoted in Carolina G. Hernandez, "The Extent of Civilian Control of the Military in the Philippines: 1946-1976" (Ph.D. dissertation, State University of New York at Buffalo, 1979), pp. 206-207.

15. Ibid., p. 211.

16. Symington Hearings, p. 355; Walden Bello and Severina Rivera, eds., *The Logistics of Repression: The Role of U.S. Assistance in Consolidating the Martial Law Regime in the Philippines* (Washington, DC: 1977), 25-26.

17. Larry A. Niksch, "The Armed Forces of the Asia Pacific Region: No. 8, The Philippines Uncertainties after the Aquino Assassination," *Pacific Defense Reporter* (February 1984): 21; estimates from the International Institute of Strategic Studies, cited by the Far Eastern Economic Review *Asia Yearbook 1983*, p. 30, in Felipe B. Miranda, "The Military in a Post-Marcos Philippines: Short-term Scenarios by a Concerned Civilian," Discussion Paper No. 84-1 (Manila: University of the Philippines, Department of Political Science, January 1984), p. 7.

18. Frederica Bunge, ed., *Philippines: A Country Study* (Washington, DC: Foreign Area Studies, American University, 1983), pp. 260-261.

19. Ibid.

20. Niksch, "Armed Forces."

21. Ferdinand E. Marcos, "The Military and National Development" (speech delivered at the graduation exercises of the 6th Regular Course, CGSC, May 28, 1974), in *Philippine Military Digest* 1:4 (1974): 3-4, quoted in Hernandez, "Extent of Civilian Control," p. 225.

22. Harold W. Maynard, *A Comparison of Military Elite Role Perceptions in Indonesia and the Philippines* (Ph.D. dissertation, American University, 1976), quoted in Miranda, "The Military," p. 3.

23. Ibid.

24. Nena Vreeland et al., *Area Handbook of the Philippines* (Washington, DC: Foreign Area Studies, American University, 1976), p. 388.

25. Lawyers Committee for International Human Rights, *The Philippines: A Country in Crisis* (New York: Lawyers Committee for International Human Rights, 1983), pp. 117-118.

26. Ibid., p. 119.

27. U.S. Congress, House, Foreign Affairs Committee, *Political Prisoners in South Vietnam and the Philippines: Hearings before the Subcommittee on Asian and Pacific Affairs*, statement of Benedict J. Kervliet, May 1, 1974, 93rd Cong., 2nd sess., May 1 and June 5, 1974, pp. 71-72.

28. *Amnesty International Report* (1982), pp. 231ff and (1981), p. 256.

29. Amnesty International, *Human Rights Violations* (1982), p. 3, and other *Amnesty International Reports*.

30. U.S. Senate, Committee on Foreign Relations, *The Situation in the Philippines: A Staff Report by Frederick Z. Brown and Carl Ford*, 98th Cong., 2nd sess., p. 33.

31. Ibid.

32. Hernandez, "Extent of Civilian Control," p. 258.

33. Quoted in Jovito R. Salonga, "The Marcos Dictatorship and a Vision of Government" (Unpublished manuscript, Los Angeles, 1984).

34. Quoted in William Butler, John Humphrey, and G. E. Bisson, *The Decline of Democracy in the Philippines* (Geneva: International Commission of Jurists, 1977), p. 7.

35. Ibid.

36. Quoted in Rolando V. del Carmen, "Constitutionality and Judicial Politics," in Rosenberg, *Marcos and Martial Law*, p. 99.

37. Bunge, *Philippines*, p. 188.

38. Ibid.

39. *Garcia Padilla v. Ponce-Enrile*, G.R. No. 61388, April 20, 1983, quoted in Lawyers Committee for International Human Rights, *The Philippines*, p. 110.

40. *New York Times*, January 27, 1973, p. 5.

41. Ferdinand E. Marcos, *The Democratic Revolution in the Philippines*, 2nd ed. (Englewood Cliffs, NJ: Prentice Hall International, 1979), p. 232.

42. Presidential Commission on Reorganization, *Organizing for Development* (Manila, 1978), quoted in Bautista, "Structure of the Philippine Administrative Systems".

43. Ledivina V. Cariño, "The Bureaucracy and Recent Developments in the Philippines" (paper presented for the 2nd Joint Seminar on U.S.-Philippine Relations, Manila, December 1983), p. 10.

44. Ibid.

45. Bautista, "Structure," pp. 8-10.

46. Ibid., p. 23.

47. Ibid.

48. Hernandez, "Extent of Civilian Control," p. 27.

49. Manuel Caoili, "Notes on Metropolitan Manila Organization," *Philippine Journal of Public Administration* 22:3 and 4 (July-October 1978): 328-349.

50. Cariño, "Bureaucracy and Recent Developments," pp. 12-16.

51. Leonor M. Briones, "The Relationship of Public Enterprise with the National Government of the Philippines" (lecture delivered at the International Seminar "The Role and Performance of Public Enterprises," Manila, June 17-28, 1985).

52. Ibid., p. 2.

53. Quoted in ibid.

54. Ibid.

55. Jonathan Kwitny, *Endless Enemies: The Making of an Unfriendly World* (New York: Congdon and Weed, 1984), p. 307.

56. Dante B. Canlas et al., *An Analysis of the Philippine Economic Crisis: A Workshop Report* (Quezon City: University of the Philippines, School of Economics, June 1984), p. 82.

57. Alfred W. McCoy, *Priests on Trial* (Australia: Penguin Books, 1984), p. 59.

Chapter 5

The Authoritarian Regime's Network of Support

Repressive regimes are undesirable, but if they enjoy the support of significant sectors of society, they are able to maintain themselves in power.

Marcos's expansion of bureaucratic power enabled him to establish the government as the key player in all aspects of Philippine life. He became the power broker, regulating the competing claims of the various powerful elites in Philippine society. Ultimately, Marcos's power rested in satisfying the rent-seeking demands of those elites; therefore, the bureaucracy took on the role of patron to the various "clients" seeking political favors. All aspects of government were connected by a web of patron-client relationships, from the leader of small villages to the top person in government: Ferdinand Marcos himself. Patrons granted favors, jobs, and prestige; in return, clients provided their support. Through those relationships, Marcos consolidated his new oligarchy. That oligarchy constituted the base of support for the Marcos regime. It consisted of the military, the technocrats and bureaucrats, businesspeople, and cronies of the president, and local leaders. Composed mainly of cabinet members and other national and local government officials, that base of support was formalized through the establishment of the dominant political party, the KBL. In its support of the Marcos government, the party united all the various elite groups; thus, Marcos's absolute power lasted for fourteen years.

Another "client" group to which Marcos needed to pay attention was foreign interests, most particularly the interests of the United States. Without the support of the United States, Marcos would have had difficulty financing domestic client groups. Marcos therefore pursued policies favorable to foreign business interests. He rhetorically claimed to be a nationalist but in practice did not behave as one. He was, in fact, richly rewarded for his support of the United States in the Vietnam War, as well as for his pursuit of policies favorable toward American investment and capital. He also used the U.S. need for military bases to secure economic and military aid for himself.

Marcos expanded, taking advantage of government authority and resources to reward his supporters. He maintained a patron-client network, and he contolled the helm.

DOMESTIC RENT SEEKERS

Consistent with the oligarchic nature of Philippine politics, Marcos used his power to reward friends and ethnic compatriots. Recipients of the rewards returned loyalty to Marcos. The reciprocal system served Marcos as a means of garnering support and institutionalizing his authoritarian system.

Marcos often used positions in the military to reward loyalty. Since his days in Congress in the 1950s, Marcos had established good relations with graduate officers from the Philippine Military Academy (PMA) and junior officers.[1] By the time he became president, those officers were in charge of the armed forces. Speaker of the House of Representatives Jose B. Laurel publicly remarked on the considerable increase of enlistees and officers from the Ilocos region, Marcos's home province. In early 1968 Laurel filed a bill in the House providing for a proportionate representation of all regions in the armed forces. The Laurel bill exposed the figures of what Senator Benigno Aquino, Jr., called the "Ilocanization of the armed forces."[2] In the year before martial law was imposed, Marcos "reshuffled field commanders to place key positions in the hands of the Ilocano officers." He was assured of their loyalty because of their ethnicity.[3] While martial law was in force, eighteen out of twenty-two PC generals were Ilocanos.

Marcos also used business as a base of patronage. He rewarded his close friends, allies, and supporters and disenfranchised his opponents. During the martial law years, Marcos established monopolies dominated by his friends and cronies. The directorates of many companies had members in common, and a substantial number of businesses had officers and connections leading to the Marcos-Romualdez families. Marcos-connected business leaders served as regional KBL leaders in their areas. Nationalizing private enterprise and the expanding government control and involvement in business enhanced the power of the Marcos regime. Centralization further increased the resources at the government's disposal.

According to John F. Doherty, Philippine business was concentrated in eighty-one families as proven by their interlocking directorates. Only 6% of their companies had public stocks. Those families can be categorized into three groups. The first group consisted of those who had accumulated wealth during the martial law years: Marcos, Romualdez, Martel, Disini, Velayo, Benedicto, Enrile, Cuenca, Silverio, Abello, Tanseco, Tantoco, Ozaeta, Oreta, and Floreindo. Those families had not been known before martial law, nor did they belong to the traditional elite. The second group consisted of the pre-martial law elite who had grown significantly under the Marcos regime: Aboitiz, Elizalde, Concepcion, Palanca, Siguion-Reyna, Alcantara, Fernandez, Nubla, Sycip-Yuchengco, and Yulo. The third group consisted of the traditional elite who had endured through the martial law years and did not suffer the fate of the Lopezes and Jacintos, who lost their wealth: Ortigas, Laurels, Zobel-Ayala, Soriano, and Madrigal.[4] The Marcos and the Romualdez families owned a long list of companies in various fields: insurance, mining, real estate, logging, gambling, farming, banking, publishing, car manufacturing, hotel and hospitality services, recording, and others.[5]

Eduardo Cojuangco and Defense Secretary Ponce-Enrile were the only two civilians in the Group of Twelve, who planned martial law. Through presidential decrees, Cojuangco and Enrile were awarded control of the coconut industry. Cojuangco was a congressman from Tarlac and a cousin of the wife of Marcos's chief rival, Benigno Aquino. Marcos supported Eduardo Cojuangco against the congressman's cousin, Jose Cojuangco, during his campaign for Congress. Jose, however, was supported by Benigno Aquino. The Cojuangco family owned Central Azucarera of Tarlac and the largest plantation, the Hacienda Luisita. Cojuangco so expanded his wealth and power during martial law that he was considered the most powerful man outside the Marcos government and a likely successor. He accumulated more farmlands and agribusiness in Luzon, Visayas, and Mindanao: 15,000 hectares of coconut land the largest cacao holdings in the country, fish ponds, and sugar plantations.[6] After Soriano's death, he took over as the chairperson of the San Miguel Corporation, a Philippine brewery.

Ponce-Enrile shared the administration of the industry as chairperson of UCPB and Unicom, and honorary chairperson of Cocofed. He was the regime's regional leader for the Cagayan Valley. He was the custom commissioner and the secretary of justice. When he lost in a senatorial election, Marcos reappointed him secretary of defense. Ponce-Enrile owned coconut and farm lands in Isabela, a logging and a match-manufacturing company. He was a director of Cuenca's PDCP and a silent partner of Angara, Abello and Associates, a law firm with large corporate accounts. His holding company was Jaka Investment Corporation. After accumulating capital, Ponce-Enrile and Cojuangco, as well as other Marcos cronies, funneled money out of the Philippines to various investments mainly in the United States.[7]

Marcos placed the sugar industry under his fraternity brother and former law classmate Roberto S. Benedicto. During Marcos's first term, he was appointed president of the Philippine National Bank (PNB). Later Marcos appointed him as Philippine ambassador to Japan, and in 1977, as the head of the Philippine Sugar Commission (Philsucom). Among other things, he owned sugar mills, the *Daily Express* (one of the largest Philippine daily newspapers), and five television and thirty-six radio stations. The media facilities were of particular interest to the government and were quickly taken over.[8] He owned shipping lines and was reported to be in control of trade with Japan. He also owned the Republic Planters Bank (RPB), which received favored treatment in 1983. The Philippine Central Bank imposed penalties on RPB for failing to meet reserve requirements. Marcos voided the penalties through the issuance of Letter of Instruction No. 1330 (June 6, 1983).[9]

Such favoritism as rescinding penalties was common in facilitating big business transactions. Another Marcos crony, Herminio Disini, married to Mrs. Marcos's cousin, Inday Escolin, received an estimated $4 million from Westinghouse for the sale of a nuclear power plant to the Philippine government. He served as the Philippine representative of the Westinghouse Power Systems Company. The Philippine plant was overpriced by at least $75 million compared to similar plants built in other countries by other companies. Marcos was instrumental in the growth of Disini's business empire, built during the martial law years. Disini's Herdis conglomerate of fifty companies had $1 billion in assets built from a monopoly of market for the cigarette filters. His competitors closed their businesses[10] after Marcos issued Presidential Decree No. 750 on July 21, 1975 "to ensure fair competition in the local cigarette industry as well as to stipulate the development and growth of the local manufacturers of cigarette filter rods."[11] That decree imposed a 100% import duty on acetate tow, the raw material used in making cigarette filters. Disini was charged only 10% import duty. In 1977 the Philippine National Bank guaranteed Herdis's loan of $25 million to buy five companies. It borrowed $25 million from foreign banks to buy Caterpillar tractors. In spite of the finance minister's objection, the loan was guaranteed by the Philippine National Bank. The loan went through on grounds of national security. Marcos stated that in case of a national emergency, the tractors could be used as tanks.

Another company with Marcos connections was the Construction Development Corporation of the Philippines (CDCP) owned by Rodolfo Cuenca. It was formed in 1966, the year Marcos was inaugurated to his first term. One of its stockholders was Pedro Valdez, Marcos's friend and the first secretary of public works.[12] The company was awarded the contract to complete the Manila North Expressway and to collect tolls for forty years to fund the project. The main government contractor for public works, CDCP later became involved in overseas operations. Another company of Cuenca, the Galleon Shipping Company, incurred $100 million dollars in government-guaranteed loans. When the company became unprofitable, it was taken over as the official Philippine container shipping company to the West Coast of the United States. In February 1983, to save CDCP's venture losses, Marcos issued an order to banks to convert its loans to equity.

Ricardo Silverio, another businessperson whose fortunes were made during martial law, was a contributor to Marcos's campaigns. He was reported as having contributed $20 million in the 1969 reelection campaign. He owned Delta Motor Sales; Toyota assembly company; Filipinas Manufacturers Bank; Delta Air; Air Manila; and had interest in textiles, logging, mining, and insurance.

Silverio, Cojuangco, and others comprised the new elite who controlled and benefited from government involvement in business. They provided the regime with a network of support and access to vast numbers of resources. In return, the regime was also ready to bail out their companies when those companies were no longer profitable. In the beginning of the 1980s, the regime rescued a number of crony-owned businesses. According to a confidential study by the U.S. embassy entitled "Creeping State Capitalism in the Philippines,"[13] the Development Bank of the Philippines (DBP) owned or managed seventy-three private companies after it had converted loans and loan guarantees of those companies to equity. The regime's involvement in business gave it the means to reward its supporters. Access to the regime was a prerequisite for business growth and survival. The resources at its disposal gave the government the capability to institutionalize its rule.

In addition to rewarding friends, Marcos allied himself with the grass roots through local and regional leaders; for example, Defense Minister Juan Ponce-Enrile was the influential leader of Cagayan Valley (Region 2), the Romaldezes in Leyte, the Duranos in Cebu, Ali Dimaporo in Lanao. They represented the Marcos government in their respective provinces by distributing favors to their constituents before elections and referendums to guarantee favorable results for the regime.

A striking example of the use of favors to influence elections is shown in the 1969 election campaign. The Board of Investments started giving aid to 107 preferred and pioneering projects, with a total sum of 1.7 billion pesos in investment of which 1.10 billion pesos would go to manufacturing, 444.2 million pesos to mining, and 154.2 million pesos to agriculture.[14] At the same time, the Marcos administration overspent millions of pesos to enhance its image and assure reelection. Marcos even availed himself of the services of American political consultants.[15] Specialized budgets, pork-barrel funds, and even departmental budgetary allocations created the most expensive election in the Philippines.[16] It is campaign overkill. The president distributed 4,000 pesos each to all barrio captains, who were the leaders of Philippine villages, or barrios, which are the smallest political units of local government. Patronage politics were oiled as insurance for grass roots support;[17] furthermore, Marcos subsidized his political allies in their individual campaigns for Senate and House seats.[18]

In Marcos's attempts to create a network of regional leaders, he had to take into account thirty powerful families scattered throughout the archipelago, families who had been key to the success of all political regimes.[19] They controlled rural banks, rice milling, trading stores, fish ponds, trucking and shipping, ice making plants, logging, land, and public offices. As such they were and still are an indispensable link between the central government and the populace. Marcos rewarded them with political positions by appointing them provincial governors, town mayors, and members of the KBL. Marcos integrated them into the national polity even as they maintained power in their respective fiefdoms. In effect, Marcos accorded legitimacy and official titles to their feudal positions.

FOREIGN RENT SEEKERS: MARCOS AND U.S. VIETNAM POLICY

The Philippine leader's constituency included U.S. government and business interests. Those interests were rooted in the "compadre colonial relations" forged during the American occupation.[20] Because of the Philippines' special ties to the U.S., a symbiotic relationship developed after Philippine independence was granted. The United States became a source of economic, political, and symbolic support. A pro-American stand also served as a symbol of legitimacy for political candidates. Such a stand assured the candidates of receiving a significant number of votes because many of Filipino voters favored things labeled "stateside" and pro-American. In return, support from the United States helped grease Philippine political machinery.[21] From President Roxas to President Marcos, the American government served as a source of support. To cut oneself off from the relationship with the United States was to cut off an umbilical cord of political patronage; in addition, one's failure to return favors would violate the Filipino cultural concept of reciprocity. As long as political and military support were provided, the United

States willingly overlooked the questionable legality of Marcos's actions. U.S. business also was willing to overlook repressive policies as long as profits were protected. Marcos granted Americans full access to the Philippine economy and enacted legislation to ensure that U.S. business operations in the Philippines would be profitable.

To further his own political ambitions, Marcos was willing to provide whatever military concessions the United States needed in return for support. His accommodation of U.S. security interests was key factor to his longevity as president. He supported the Vietnam war but at the same time was careful not to alienate or earn the ire of Filipino nationalists as well as that of critics of the war.[22] In fact, Marcos's position on the war shifted to suit his political whims. In debate on a 1964 bill to send troops to Vietnam, then-senator Marcos vehemently opposed the bill, which passed the House of Representatives, dominated by Liberals, but failed to get through the Senate. As a presidential candidate, Marcos said:

History shows that every nation that fell to communism owed its defeat not to foreign invasion but to disintegration from within through the failure of its leadership and its institutions. The sending of combat troops will commit our country to war without regard for the provision of our Constitution for a declaration of war, and in the face of the express mandate in which we renounce war as an instrument of national policy. What South Vietnam needs is the will to fight which cannot be exported. It [Philippine-American friendship] will be served today and in the future by Filipino leaders who act with becoming dignity and maturity as well as [with] true goodwill toward America, rather than those who miss no chance to help their loyalty and manifest canine devotion which only results in embarrassing America no less than the Philippines before the world.[23]

Immediately after he was inaugurated, however, Marcos changed his position and worked for the passage of the Vietnam-aid bill. After cabinet discussions and negotiations with U.S. officials, especially with the Joint United States Military Advisory Group, the Vietnam-aid bill entitled "An Act Appropriating Funds to Increase Philippine Economic and Technical Assistance to South Vietnam" was certified by Marcos to the Philippine Congress on February 17, 1966. The bill called for the appropriation of thirty-five million pesos or approximately $9 million "to increase Philippine economic and technical assistance to South Vietnam by sending an engineer construction battalion composed of volunteers with the necessary security to Vietnam."[24] Marcos's change of position began a long period of Marcos accommodation of American military and political interests in Southeast Asia.

In September 1966 President Lyndon B. Johnson received Marcos in a state visit. In a White House reception and dinner, Johnson praised Marcos's career as a guerrilla chief during World War II for which he won two Silver Stars and a Distinguished Service Cross. The American president also recalled that just a few days before, on Marcos's forty-ninth birthday, "[two-thousand] Filipino troops began their journey to Vietnam to take their place beside Australians, Koreans, New Zealanders, Americans, and South Vietnamese." He added that Marcos was "the symbol of the undaunted spirit in Asia that is enlarging liberty and enhancing the lives of human beings."[25]

Marcos praised the United States for inspiring and imparting freedom and democracy to the world and to the Philippines in particular. He called upon the United States to carry the burden of leadership in Asia and not to abandon the cause of democracy against the rising tide of communism in Asia, as in the case of China. Marcos also pointed to the danger of what he called a "security gap" in Asia, which "invites intervention, subversion, and foreign inspired wars of liberation." That dangerous security gap could be filled only by America, however much Asian nations abhorred, or at best regarded with distrust, such non-Asian power. Marcos stated that only American military power was acceptable in Asia, for only America was great enough to deter Communist China's aggressive tendencies.[26]

Marcos gave the Johnson government its support in its involvement in Vietnam. To Marcos, American policy was consonant with containing and discouraging the Communist threat, infiltration, subversion, and aggression. Making clear the American aims in Indochina, he stated that "Americans and their Government should never tire of repeating that the United States is in Vietnam for the purpose of assisting that nation in defending its independence and territorial integrity.[27] According to Marcos, American presence in Vietnam also "provided, though unintentionally, encouragement and support to those who successfully resisted the attempted Communist take-over in Indonesia."[28]

In exchange for supporting American policy, Marcos received economic and military aid. In a brief remark about Filipino World War II veterans' benefits, Marcos complained that

after the war we have had to endure American ridicule for our claims to equal rights under the veterans law of [the United States]. We were unprepared for the rebuffs that we received but even less prepared for the hostility in attitudes of some of your executive officials who have had to deal with us. Our former common enemy, Japan, had been patient and understanding. From you, our allies, we expected nothing less. But we did not get it.[29]

The subject of veterans' claims for compensation was discussed during the state visit. President Johnson assured Marcos of his support for legislation "to provide increased benefits to Philippine veterans, their widows, orphans, and other dependents."[30] The two presidents also agreed that "their representatives would discuss the means of restoring wartime pay to those recognized Philippine guerrillas who did not previously receive it and compensating members of the Philippine Army for erroneous deductions of advanced salary for their wartime pay." This response received positive reception from guerrillas and their organizations in the Philippines.

The fifteenth item in the Joint Communique referred to defense. President Johnson announced that the United States would expand civic action capabilities of the Philippine army by providing equipment to five engineering battalions during the fiscal year and would do the same to five more the following year. The delivery of a destroyer escort for the Philippine navy was anticipated. In a more comprehensive manner, Johnson called for the continuing review of the U.S. Military Assistance Program "to ensure that the material and training supplied to the Philippine armed forces were kept appropriate to the changing requirements and missions of these forces."[31]

Marcos returned to the Philippines triumphantly. He earned greater prestige at home for getting an audience with the American people. Marcos became even more popular among Filipinos after the American president called him his "right arm in Asia."

To reciprocate the warm White House reception, the following month Marcos invited the American president to Manila. He hosted the 1966 summit conference of heads of allied states participating in the war in Indochina. American allies in Asia, South Vietnam, South Korea, Australia, and New Zealand accepted the invitation to attend the conference during which the attendees hoped to evaluate the prospects for negotiations and to review the military, economic, and political situation in Vietnam. Senator J. William Fulbright voiced strong criticism against the conference, asserting that it would not be productive and claiming that for such a conference to be effective, the bombing of North Vietnam must be halted without waiting for assurances of corresponding deescalation from the North. He also stated that the conference should include India, Pakistan and Japan. According to the *New York Times*, Fulbright implied that Marcos invited and offered to host the conference in repayment for American promises of increased aid. The senator remarked, "Mr. Marcos was well-paid so he ought to respond."[32] According to White House Press Secretary Bill Moyers, Marcos discussed the conference with Johnson but did not propose a date. Critics of Johnson's visit to the Philippines and of the summit conference alleged that it was to Johnson's political advantage to show his desire for peace before the November congressional election. Gerald Ford, Republican leader of the House, was also suspicious of Johnson's domestic political motive.[33]

A veteran observer of Philippine-American affairs, Claude Buss remarked that Marcos would enjoy the limelight and put "American aid in his pocket." Marcos played his role with consummate skill with an eye on his own political future.[34] Clearly the summit conference was again another boost to Marcos's domestic and international image and political career.

Allied leaders received a tumultuous welcome in the tradition of Philippine hospitality and in the spirit of Marcos's ostentation. Fiestas (traditional feasts in honor of Catholic patron saints) were held in honor of guests. Even a *sabong*, a Filipino cockfight, was held to amuse the visiting dignitaries. Amidst the rousing reception were demonstrators who protested against Johnson's Vietnam policy. Demonstrators clashed with police outside the Manila hotel where the Johnsons were billeted. Around 2,000 people staged an anti-Vietnam war, anti-Johnson rally. Some twenty students were arrested and twelve were injured in the clash.[35]

In addition to the political and diplomatic show of support, Marcos sent the Philippine Civic Action Group (Philcag) to participate in the war. Jointly financed by the Philippine and American governments, Philcag was a battalion composed of engineers to work on infrastructure projects and a security force. Philcag's funding was clouded in secrecy. For many reasons, the manner of financing the contingent was not made clear to the public. One reason was pride and shame or the Filipino concept of *hiya*. Another was the question of legality. When the truth came out, in the hearings of the U.S. Senate's Foreign Relations Committee, that Philcag was being funded secretly by the United States and that its accounting was shrouded in mystery, Philcag became a liability to Philippine as well as to American authorities.[36] Philcag's involvement in Vietnam paved the way for greater American support to the Philippine armed forces through regular channels of aid as well as through Vietnam-related expenses of the Department of National Defense of the U.S. government.

Marcos pushed hard for a bill to send Philcag to Vietnam. When it passed, the United States agreed to do the following:

1. To equip Philcag in Vietnam temporarily and to provide logistical support.

2. To pay overseas allowances, over and above the regular pay to be provided by the Philippine government.

3. To provide replacement costs for a replacement unit in the Philippines.

4. To supply two Swiftcraft in addition to two committed earlier without relation to Philcag. (A Swiftcraft is a river-patrol craft about fifty feet in length.)

5. To accelerate funding in fiscal year 1966 for equipment for three engineer construction battalions previously considered for later financing under the military assistance program.

6. To supply M-14 rifles and M-60 machine guns for one battalion combat team to be funded in fiscal year 1966.

The above items were to be paid for from service funds of the Department of Defense as Vietnam-related costs and not from the Military Assistance Program.[37]

In relation to Philcag negotiations, the first three items were not initially sought by the Marcos government. Immediately after Marcos was inaugurated as president, the Philippine government requested rifles, machine guns, two Swiftcrafts, and accelerated funding for the fiscal year 1966 to pay for the three engineer construction battalions. The two Swiftcrafts would be used for antismuggling campaigns because they were small, fast, and efficient. The engineer battalions were tasked with construction of infrastructure such as roads, bridges, and schools. The United States eventually supplied seven more battalions making a total of ten equipped contingents.

An aggregate of more than $38 million was spent for funding Philcag and for the subsequent military assistance to the Philippines. Marcos clearly benefited, but Philippine involvement in the Vietnam War through Philcag continued to cause controversy. The emerging militant, antiwar movement in many parts of the world, including the Philippines, made the war an issue. Opponents from the left as well as from the right coalesced on the issue. Both liberals and conservatives joined in a chorus of criticism on the futility of a war against national liberation or self-determination.

Philippine politics was not spared from the pressures of the antiwar movement. Supporters of nationalism and anti-Americanism in the Philippines became more vocal and militant in intellectual and academic circles, in the press, and in Congress, until Marcos, in his bid for reelection, had to justify Philippine involvement in Vietnam. In response to the imminent withdrawal of the United States from Vietnam, Marcos became a nationalist. He adopted development as the centerpiece of his foreign policy for his second term. He appointed as foreign-affairs secretary Carlos P. Romulo, once president of the United Nations General Assembly and former ambassador to the United States. Marcos hoped to benefit from Romulo's prestige because Romulo had held numerous important positions both national and international.

Following his reelection on November 11, 1969, Marcos withdrew the Philcag detachment from Vietnam; however, the controversy surrounding Philippine involvement in the war did not end. On November 19 all the transcripts from the Senate Subcommittee on U.S. Security Agreements and Commitments Abroad were published. Senator William J. Fulbright, chairman of the U.S. Senate Foreign Relations Committee publicly stated that Philcag worked as a mercenary group "under corrupt terms and administration." It was alleged that the battalion was funded to show that Johnson's policy was being wholeheartedly supported in Asia. Fulbright described the U.S.-Philippine agreement on Philcag as "the ultimate corruption" and said it was "illusory" for the United States to "make deals like this in an effort to create the impression that Asian allies supported the United States involvement in Vietnam."[38] The Marcos administration had feared that criticism would be directed against its Vietnam deals and therefore avoided comment about the financing of Philcag.

James P. Wilson, deputy chief of mission at the U.S. embassy in the Philippines, remarked in the hearing that

since the Marcos administration did not want the Philippine contingent to be tagged by critics as a mercenary group, they have desired that all the assistance to Philcag be kept quiet as possible. . . . Marcos' opponents, however, kept raising the question as to how the Philippine contingency was financed. During the years since 1966, Marcos had attempted to keep the Philcag issue from becoming a political liability.[39]

Student groups continually demonstrated and rallied during the first months of 1970, adding to the sharp criticisms and pointed remarks of Fulbright, Wilson, and Symington during the Senate hearings:

Fulbright: My own feeling is that all we did was go over and hire their soldiers in order to support our then administration's view that so many people were in sympathy with our war in Vietnam. And we paid a very high price for it. That is my own view.[40]

Fulbright: Why do the Philippines insist on a price for sending Philcag if there is no great love and/or sympathetic opinion for the United States? Why do they still insist on it? Why did they not send it without insisting on a price? . . . We have already given them hundreds of millions of dollars in other areas that had nothing to do with this. I remember having a hearing in 1963 involving a bill which was passed in the Congress giving the Philippine government $73 million for war damage claims of individuals. But Philippine interest groups sent a substantial amount of money, who with their ambassadors distributed it very wisely among Members of our Congress.[41]

Wilson: I hope this subcommittee does not have the opinion that every Filipino is a crook. This is not the case and there are a great number of very fine people in that country.[42]

Symington: Speaking of Paree, they are being continually informed of progress in the Paris talks, and apparently would like a role in the eventual Vietnam settlement. We have lost to date 1,054 boys killed from my state. The Filipinos have lost eight plus 17 wounded. Without any criticism of the executive branch, there was a big meeting of all those helping us in Vietnam. The Philippines was prominently represented. There was a lot of fanfare about it. If the Philippine nation desires to participate in the ultimate settlement, if they believe as General Romulo said yesterday on television it is important for us to stand firmly united in Vietnam and because of the tens of millions of dollars this war has put in their country it seems to me they might consider not withdrawing the remaining 1,500 noncombat people out of their 37 million population.[43]

More criticism arose during the middle of March 1971. Symington appeared on the program *Face the Nation*, where he remarked that Philcag "was a pretty shoddy story" and alluded to its misuse by the Marcos government.[44] According to Symington, the key question in the issue was who got the money. The senator was referring to how much support the United States gave to the Philippine unit in Vietnam, which was four times the amount given by the Philippine government, in addition to other aid received by the Philippine government from the United States. Philippine military authorities denied the allegations about the degree of U.S. support. Senator Salvador Laurel of the Philippines contributed to the Symington hearings by making inquiries of the Philippine military. In reply, the secretary of national defense, Juan Ponce-Enrile, the AFP chief of staff, General Manuel Yan, and Philcag's deputy commander, General Eduardo Garcia said in separate testimony that there had been no monetary assistance from the United States.[45]

Even before the inquiries were held in November 1969, the Malacanang Palace press office issued this statement: "The Philippines received no fee nor payment of any kind in support of Philcag, or its personnel, nor has there been any grant given in consideration of sending the Philcag to Vietnam."[46]

On March 25 the results of the General Accounting Office investigation were revealed by Symington. Controller General Elmer B. Staats verified that American assistance was a quid pro quo for the deployment of Philcag to South Vietnam. The General Accounting Office report outlined the financial breakdown as well as the pay and allowances of the Philippine contingent. It also noted that the investigation was "seriously hampered by the reluctance of the Departments of State and Defense to give access to documents."[47]

What happened to the money paid for in quarterly payments between October 1966 and October 1969 could not be established. Symington showed a photocopy of a check for $338,219.60 payable to the secretary of defense of the Philippines. It was also shown that the checks were endorsed by Ernesto S. Mata, the secretary of defense. The checks were usually deposited at the Camp Aguinaldo (the headquarters of the Philippine army) branch of the Philippine Veterans Bank (PVB).[48] How the money was disbursed and if it was received by the Philcag contingent could not be established. In the face of the evidence, Mata denied that the money was connected to Philcag. The money given to the Philippine government was, he said, part of "intelligence funds for national security."[49] Philippine Congress members proposed that an inquiry be conducted into how the funds were spent. Senator Laurel asked: "Where did we use it? . . . Did we use it to finance a project on national security and intelligence? If so, what were these projects?"[50] Marcos, by contrast, brushed aside the issue. He said that it was "not important enough to affect relations between the two countries (i.e., between the Philippines and the United States)." He said: "It's a small matter; let's leave it at that."[51] He benefited from the Philcag deal and was able to defuse opponents' criticisms.

Marcos emerged unscathed from the imbroglio primarily because the United States willingly overlooked corruption in exchange for political support and use of Philippine military bases.

MARCOS AND U.S. STRATEGIC INTEREST

The Americans felt uncomfortable because of the corruption and human rights violations of the Marcos's government, and they were aware of the contradiction his actions posed to the purported democratic values of America. Despite its altruistic concerns, however, the United States was focused on security, and in the end security concerns governed U.S. policy. The military bases in the Philippines most interested American policy makers. According to a congressional report in 1972:

In both Korea and the Philippines, then, US policy appears to be in transition from the idealism of the past, based on an assumption that American democracy could and should be adopted by others, to a new pragmatism. At that time, in both countries we appear to be immobilized by our own presence and by commitments which Presidents Park and Marcos are able to use as leverage in obtaining from us what they want, . . . turning their weakness into assets in dealing with us as patron and protector.[52]

America's desire to maintain its presence in the Philippines, as in Korea, created ambivalence in policy. Larry Niksch and Marjorie Niehaus of the Congressional Research Service of the Library of Congress delineated four alternative strategies for the United States in dealing with the Marcos regime. The first two strategies assumed that the United States would emphasize its regional security objectives and its strategic policy. The second two assumed that at least equal priority would be given to human rights and political evolution.[53]

1. The progovernment strategy: The United States will give both material and symbolic assistance to Marcos in return for a guarantee from him for the continued use of U.S. bases in the Philippines so that the United States can maintain its policy in Asia and the Indian Ocean. This strategy assumed that the interest of the United States was best served through the status quo, namely, that

stability and order be preserved in the Philippines for economic growth. Communication with the opposition would occur for information-gathering purposes only.

2. The strategy of equilibrium: The United States would avoid only certain symbols of open support for the internal policies of the Marcos regime but would continue to support the regime by providing military and economic aid. Human rights would be mentioned only through quiet diplomacy and in private government-to-government dealings. The opposition would not be encouraged to use violent confrontation with the regime, and communication with it would be maintained.

3. The strategy of distancing: This strategy involved public criticism of the Marcos regime and its violations of civil liberties and human rights. "Distancing" would include a neutral attitude toward limited congressional cuts in aid, thus increasing scrutiny of any aid request from the Philippines. Distancing would risk America's bases in the Philippines. The United States would encourage violent confrontation among opponents to the Marcos government.

4. The strategy of confrontation: According to Niksch and Niehaus, "this would entail putting the Philippine government on notice that failure to alter general policies affecting democratic political development and human rights would result in significant reductions in U.S. security assistance."

Open confrontation would most likely entail the highest risk of retaliation against U.S. bases and strengthen opponents to the government in their actions and demands.[54]

A released top-secret document provided some caution in emphasizing the latter two strategies. George F. Kennan, one of the formulators of U.S. policy after World War II, stated:

We have fifty percent of the world's wealth. But only 6.3 percent of its population. This disparity is particularly great between ourselves and the people of Asia. In this situation we cannot fail to be the object of envy and resentment. Our real task is to devise a pattern of relationships which will permit us to maintain this position of disparity without positive detriment to our national security. We will have to dispense with all sentimentality and daydreaming. And our attention will have to be concentrated everywhere on our immediate national objectives. We need not deceive ourselves that we can afford today the luxury of world benefaction. We should cease to talk about vague, and for the Far East, unreal objectives such as human rights, the raising of living standards, and democratization. We should recognize that our influence in the Pacific and the Far Eastern world are absolutely vital to our security. And we should concentrate our policy on seeing to it that those areas remain in hands which we can rely on. It is my own guess on the basis of such study as we have given the problem so far Japan and the Philippines will be found to be the cornerstone of such a Pacific security system. And if we can contrive to maintain effective control over these areas there can be no serious threat to our security from the East within our time.[55]

United States policy toward Marcos through five administrations from Johnson to Reagan had supported strategy toward Marcos. Their reasons varied, but all essentially revolved around the Philippine role in U.S. security.[56] Johnson wanted Marcos's support for the United States in the Vietnam War. In exchange for sending the Philcag contingency to Vietnam, Marcos received considerable aid to strengthen the Philippine military. The Nixon administration wanted allied countries to assume a larger role in the defense of allied interests. Withdrawing from mainland Southeast Asia made U.S. military bases in the Philippines more critical if the United States was to continue to be a Pacific power. In 1975 President Gerald Ford reemphasized the American commitment to the maintenance of "equilibrium in the Pacific" and to the stability and security of states in the region. He said: "There [was] to be no withdrawal from Asia to a 'fortress America.'" Because this was announced after his visit to China, the doctrine emphasized increasing cooperation among the United States, China, and other Asian countries. U.S. bases in the Philippines were pivotal in implementing this doctrine in a security strategy.[57]

The U.S. military bases in the Philippines were considered essential to the U.S. government's strategic policy of projecting power in Asia and the Pacific. The location of those bases provided commanding control and access as well as support for allied forces from the Pacific to the Indian Ocean and to the Persian Gulf. American foreign-policy makers had always perceived that the strategic location of the bases and their continued use by the United States provided regional stability to its allies in Asia, protected sea lanes and trade routes in Asia and the Pacific, and made possible military readiness and immediate response to crises in the area. The combined air and naval bases "complement[ed] each other to such an extent that their . . . contribution to military effectiveness is greater than their contributions taken separately."[58]

Several studies concluded that alternatives or any combination of alternatives to the bases of Clark and Subic Bay would be less effective and more expensive. According to Admiral Robert L. J. Long, U.S. Navy commander-in-chief in the Pacific, duplicating those bases would cost the United States approximately $3 billion to $4 billion.[59]

Clark Air Base was the headquarters of the Thirteenth Air Force and a support facility for the Fifth Air Force operating out of Japan. The facilities at Clark included Crow Valley Weapons Range for training and missile firing-ranges; gunnery practice fields; and an electronic warfare range, Wallace Air Station, which provided major radar and communication facilities. There was also Camp John Hay Air Base Leave and Recreation Center in Baguio City. Subic Naval Base, the operational base for the carrier task force of the Seventh Fleet, serviced and repaired 60% of U.S. naval vessels. It had the largest naval supply depot for oil, petroleum and other lubricants, and ammunition storage. It included the naval air station in Cubi Point and the San Miguel Naval Communications Station. The San Miguel Station and Clark had facilities that included the satellite surveillance system aimed at the Soviets.

In 1980 about 14,000 permanent U.S. military personnel were stationed at Clark and Subic, and an average of 9,000 sailors and marines were in port at any given time. The estimate did not include U.S. civilian employees and about 20,000

Filipino personnel.[60] The bases were the second largest employers in the country next to the Philippine government.

Even with the dictatorial powers of Marcos in place, because of the importance of the bases, the United States followed a mix of the first two alternative policies outlined by Niksch and Niehaus. Secretary of State Henry Kissinger, vicar of foreign policy during the Nixon-Ford years, refused to submit a human rights assessment to Congress until 1977. Kissinger prescribed that "the United States should not harass [our] authoritarian friends . . . , for they may become humane because [of] their internal dynamic; communist totalitarians, on the other hand, are morally worse than authoritarians and will not evolve in a human direction." It was therefore not sound policy to pressure the friendly, anticommunist, authoritarian government. Kissinger's view did not differ from Ambassador Jean Kirkpatrick's delineation of authoritarian and totalitarian governments, an assessment that had wide acceptance in the Reagan administration.[61]

During the first three years of martial law, American military aid increased considerably, by 106 percent, compared to the three years preceding it. Military aid jumped from $80.8 million to $166.3 million. American economic aid rose sharply, too. Economic assistance also brought planes outfitted with machine guns; these were used by the armed forces to bring troops to Mindanao.[62]

The Carter administration had the most vocal and explicit pronouncements on human rights. Secretary of State Cyrus Vance stated that human rights were to be a cornerstone of U.S. foreign policy. Vance's assistant, Warren Christopher, did not see any contradiction between human rights and security policies in the long run. He said:

Our strength as a Nation, our magnetism to the world at large are predicated on our commitment to human rights. The pursuit of this cause is not an ideological luxury cruise with no practical port of call. Our idealism and our self-interest coincide. Widening the circle of countries which share our human rights values is at the very core of our security interest. Such nations make strong allies. Their commitment to human rights gives them an inner strength and stability which causes them to stand steadfastly with us on the most difficult issues of our time.[63]

Carter's human rights policy made the Marcos government cautious. The United States interceded on behalf of some of Marcos's human rights victims. When Trinidad Herrera, one of the leaders of the urban poor in Manila, was put into prison, US embassy officials interceded. The Carter administration also expressed its objection by abstaining from voting on some requests for loans from international institutions that loaned money to the Philippines. For example, because of Marcos's human rights record, the United States abstained on six industrial loans from the World Bank and the Asian Development Bank.[64]

In December 1979 the Soviets invaded Afghanistan. President Carter considered the invasion one of the greatest crises since World War II. In his State of the Union Message in 1980, he expressed the need to increase American military strength and project its power to prevent and contain Soviet aggression in the region and to be able to respond to upheaval in the Gulf states. The Carter doctrine made the Persian

Gulf a vital interest to the United States because of its oil supplies. According to the president, "The denial of these oil supplies, to us or to others, would threaten our security and provoke an economic crisis greater than that of the Great Depression . . . , with a fundamental change in the way we live."[65]

The Carter doctrine heightened the significance of the U.S. bases in the Philippines, which also coincided with the review of the Military Bases Agreement. Assistant Secretary for East Asian and Pacific Affairs Richard Holbrooke stated before the hearings in Congress that the United States was "obviously troubled by human rights abuses in the Philippines. However, we don't believe that security and economic assistance should be reduced because of human rights problems . . . [T]he Philippines has strategic importance, not only for our own country, but also for nations friendly to the United States in the region, and thus we should continue our support.[66]

The Reagan administration pursued the policy of asserting American power. During previous administrations, American power adjusted to certain limits and to the mutual interests of the United States and the Soviet Union[67] in order to maintain detente between the superpowers and to pursue the strategic balance. Perceiving a greater Soviet threat than earlier administrations, the Reagan White House sought to assert American superiority and to broaden the perimeters of national security; thus, it put a higher priority on defense. The military bases in the Philippines were essential to strengthening national security; consequently, the Reagan administration adopted the first policy alternative to the Philippines, the progovernment strategy. Thus both material and symbolic gestures were provided by the Reagan administration to Marcos, whom the American president called as "a voice of reason and moderation in international forums."[68]

A string of high U.S. officials—Secretaries Alexander Haig, Caspar Weinberger, and George Shultz—visited the Philippines. Vice-President George Bush praised Marcos during his 1981 inauguration saying, "We love your adherence to democratic processes."[69] Marcos was then granted a state visit to the United States in September 1982, his second since 1966. Ronald Reagan received Marcos warmly. Support for the Marcos government manifested itself in the negotiation of an extradition treaty and in the expeditious review of the Military Bases Agreement. In the renegotiation, concluded in April 1983, $900 million was promised by the Reagan administration to assist the Marcos government, almost twice what the Carter administration promised in the previous five years. In exchange for aid, Marcos guaranteed the United States "unhampered military operations of its forces in the Philippines."[70]

AMERICAN BUSINESS IN THE PHILIPPINES

In 1947 an amendment known as the "parity ordinance" or the "parity amendment" was appended to the Philippine Constitution. According to Article XIII,

Section 1 (Conservation and Utilization of Natural Resources) of the Philippine Constitution:

All agricultural, timber and mineral lands of public domain, waters, minerals, coal, petroleum, and other mineral oils, all forces and sources of potential energy, and other natural resources of the Philippines belong to the State, and their disposition, exploitation, development, or utilization shall be limited to citizens of the Philippines or corporations or associations at least sixty per centrum of the capital of which is owned by such citizens, subject to any existing right, grant, lease, or concession at the time of the inauguration of the Government established under this Constitution. Natural resources, with the exception of public agricultural land, shall not be alienated, and no license, concession, or lease for the exploitation, development, or utilization of any of the natural resources shall be granted for a period exceeding twenty-five years, renewable for another twenty-five years, except as to water rights for irrigation, water supply, fisheries, or industrial uses other than the development of water power, in which cases beneficial use may be the measure and the limit of the grant.[71]

The ordinance was amended to grant citizens of the United States the same privileges and rights Philippine citizens enjoyed. According to the Second Ordinance appended to the Philippine Constitution:

Notwithstanding the provision of Section One, Article Thirteen, and Section Eight, Article Fourteen, of the [foregoing] Constitution, during the affectivity of the Executive Agreement entered into by the President of the Philippines with the President of the United States on the fourth of July, nineteen hundred and forty-six, pursuant to the provisions of the Commonwealth Act Number Seventeen hundred and thirty-three, but in no case to extend beyond the third of July, nineteen hundred and seventy-four, the disposition, exploitation, development and utilization of all agricultural, timber and mineral lands of public domain, waters, minerals, coals, petroleum, and other mineral oils, all forces and sources of potential energy and other natural resources of the Philippines, and the operation of public utilities, shall, if open to any person, be open to citizens of the United States and to all forms of business enterprise owned and controlled, directly or indirectly by citizens of the United States in the same manner as to, and under the same conditions imposed upon, citizens of the Philippines or corporations or associations owned or controlled by citizens of the Philippines.[72]

The amendment was hotly contested in the Philippine Congress. The Nacionalistas and the Liberals voted to unseat Luis Taruc and his Democratic Alliance, which consisted of three senators and eight representatives, to minimize opposition to the amendment.[73] President Manuel Roxas tried to get the amendment passed by Congress and then by the general public. On September 16, 1946, Paul V. McNutt, the U.S. high commissioner to the Philippines and subsequently U.S. ambassador to the Philippines, cabled Washington that Roxas was "devoting every effort [to] secure requisite majority [of] both house[s] for [the] equal rights amendment [to the] Constitution."[74] A technical question about the counting of votes had to be brought to the Supreme Court, which also denied the questions about parity. Two-thirds of the qualified voters went to the polls and passed the parity provision in March 1947.[75]

The adoption of the amendment conformed to a tradition of concessions to U.S. business, and the concessions were always controversial. Several cases were brought to court during the pre-martial law days in order to determine exactly what rights Americans had under Philippine law. The Supreme Court took a restrictive view of those rights, and in every case Marcos intervened to countermand the effect of the Supreme Court ruling to allay the fears of American business.

In 1954 William H. Quasha bought a 2,616-square-meter parcel of land on Makati's millionaire row called Forbes Park. Quasha asked the courts whether he could continue to own the land after 1974. In 1969 the Court of First Instance of Rizal Province ruled that when parity ceased to be in effect on July 3, 1974, "what must be considered to end should be the right to acquire land, and not the right to continue ownership of land already acquired prior to that time." The lower court ruled on the basis of the "vested rights" theory.[76] Also at stake in the ruling were some 7,000 hectares of land, including an area of more than 13,000 square meters of corporate lands and more than 12,000 square meters of agricultural lands.

In *Republic of the Philippines and/or Solicitor General v. William H. Quasha*, G.R. No. L-30299, August 17, 1972, the Supreme Court reversed the lower court's decision. It ruled that the rights granted to citizens of the United States are subject to definite resolutory terms. The Supreme Court reiterated that parity right is "in no case to extend beyond the third of July, 1974."[77] Land acquired by Americans since the time of Philippine independence in 1946, valued between $50 million to $100 million, was subject to the Supreme Court decision.

The termination of ownership shocked the American community in Manila. As a consequence of the decision, seven bills designed to implement the court ruling were introduced in the Philippine Congress. Senator Arturo Tolentino called for the confiscation without compensation of all lands owned by Americans. To allay fears and to calm the American community, Marcos announced that his government would give just and fair compensation to Americans who surrendered ownership of property they held as required by the Supreme Court decision. He explained that he opposed nationalist legislators' demand that American holdings be confiscated without the benefits of compensation.[78]

The second landmark case affecting U.S.-Philippine economic relations was the *Luzon Stevedoring Company (Luzteveco) v. Anti-Dummy Board*. That case ruling prohibited foreigners from being members of the boards of directors or managers in industry and business and reserved the positions for citizens of the Philippines; therefore, American citizens would be barred from controlling their subsidiaries through contracts or through managerial positions.[79]

The third case dealt with an important sector of the Philippine economy: retail trade. Most Filipinos from all walks of life, in urban areas as well as rural areas, depend on "*sari-sari*" (literally, "mix-mix") stores for daily grocery needs. In the interest of giving more opportunities to Filipino entrepreneurs, who were usually behind Chinese and Americans in business, the Retail Trade Nationalization Act, or Republic Act No. 1180, was passed by the Philippine Congress in 1954. The act was to take effect on June 18, 1964, ten years after the law's passage "in order to give the foreign business establishments enough time to make certain adjustments."[80] The law "prohibited persons who are not citizens of the Philippines, as well as corporations or partnerships not wholly owned by Filipino citizens, from engaging directly or indirectly in the retail business."[81] Teofilo Reyes, Jr., the Philippine secretary of commerce ruled that only wholly owned Filipino establishments could operate when the Nationalization Law took effect. Twenty-three cases were brought before the court. President Johnson wrote President Diosdado Macapagal and warned him that "the arbitrary enforcement of the retail trade law might adversely affect the mutual interest of both countries."[82]

In view of the Second Ordinance appended to the Philippine Constitution and the Laurel-Langley Agreement of 1954, it was argued that Americans had the right to engage in retail trade and were exempt from the law. Meanwhile American businesspeople did not like the law and branded it "anti-American." President Johnson exerted pressure on their behalf. In the Joint Communique issued on the occasion of President Macapagal's visit to the United States, the American president stated that the "United States' economic relations with the Philippines would be seriously impaired if an enforcement of the Philippine Retail Trade Nationalization Law were to prejudice the position of long-established American firms."[83] The Solicitor General of the Macapagal administration issued a statement asserting that the government had "committed itself to the policy of exempting American business firms from the operation of the Retail Trade Law."[84]

The Philippine Packing Corporation and several other American firms sought court action to bring the conflicting views to a resolution. Judge Hilarion Jarencio of the Court of First Instance of Manila ruled on December 16, 1966, that American corporations and business enterprises "are prohibited by the Retail Trade Nationalization Law from engaging in retail business." Retail trade was defined by law as "sales in limited quantities to the general public of consumer goods for personal or household consumption and also [as] sales for industrial or commercial consumption." As Fernandez thus aptly summarized, retail trade is "any sale by a producer to a consumer, regardless of volume and whatever the end-use."[85] On the basis of the ruling, a large number of American companies such as Procter and Gamble, the Philippine Education Company, Eastman Kodak, Smith Bell, and Singer Sewing Machine would be affected.

In a related move, Mayor Antonio J. Villegas of the city of Manila confirmed "that he would not renew licenses for American businesses when they expire December 31."[86] The mayor and the city government's Better Business Bureau started an inquiry into the legal implications of the court's decision. It also looked into the citizenship of the controlling interest of business establishments in Manila. The possibility was raised that sales of newspapers and leases of movies or films might also be subject to the court's ruling.

Meanwhile, American businesses, led by Esso Standard, Caltex, Tidewater Oil, and Burroughs Limited, became concerned with the consequences of the ruling and so they appealed directly to Marcos; the Philippine Packing Corporation, in contrast, appealed to the Supreme Court.[87] In response, Marcos issued an executive order exempting American firms from the Retail Trade Nationalization Law by virtue of the nonabridgement clause of the Laurel-Langley Agreement provided they comply with the requirements of reciprocity. Villegas filed a petition in Supreme Court to void the president's order. Meanwhile, fifteen American firms had suspended their operations on January 1, 1967.

On January 18, 1967, the Philippine Supreme Court ruled that Villegas must abide by the executive order promulgated by Marcos and denied as well as dismissed the petition filed by the mayor. In a unanimous ruling, the court sustained the executive order "unless and until voided or modified by final judgment of a competent court in appropriate cases." The court also declared that the president's decisions were binding upon local officials.[88] The Supreme Court upheld the presidential order; however, it left open the question of the interpretation of the Retail Trade Nationalization Law. Earlier petitions of some twenty cases for declaratory relief by several American companies were understood to have been answered.

The Supreme Court focused its decisions on the question of jurisdiction, namely, that of a local official, a city mayor, in relation to the president; but it did not offer a conclusive nationalist decision on the Retail Trade Nationalization. The court instead offered two conflicting approaches or responses. The mayor of Manila registered a response in opposition to Marcos's executive order.[89] The president's order showed his favoritism toward foreign businesses, he said. Under martial law, foreign businesses would find a better ally in Marcos because he could issue decrees in their favor. When an authoritarian system was imposed, his action went beyond the purview of the courts, legislature, and local politicians.

If Marcos was accommodating to U.S. interests before martial law, afterward he became more so. In the late 1960s and early 1070s, the American role in the Philippines was increasingly scrutinized by Nationalist critics. In view of the seeming disarray of conflicting ideologies and growing nationalism, Marcos assured the protection of U.S. interest in the Philippines. The United States saw Marcos as a reliable ally; in return, Marcos received U.S. support. Under martial law, the stable appearance of the government reassured foreign interests. American businesspeople viewed martial law as a welcomed relief from the growing uncertainties of business relationships, and martial law did not threaten U.S. military and strategic interests. With Marcos in power, the retention and continued support of American military bases was ensured. Marcos also enunciated policies favorable to U.S. needs.

It was indeed true that neither U.S. citizens nor businesses were endangered by martial law; in fact, U.S. business interests welcomed martial law in the Philippines. According to *Time Magazine*, "In a telegram to Malacanang Palace, the U.S. Chamber of Commerce in Manila, forgetting its manners as a foreign guest, effusively praised Marcos' program."[90] It was widely believed that that telegram was the first message of congratulations to Marcos. The telegram stated:

The American Chamber of Commerce wishes you every success in your endeavor to restore peace and order, business confidence, economic growth and [the] well-being of the Filipino people and nation. We assure you of our confidence and cooperation in achieving these objectives. We are communicating the feelings of our associates and affiliates in the United States.[91]

The American Chamber of Commerce telegram was by no means for public relations only. The enthusiasm and well wishes for Marcos were based on the American businesspeople's perception that Marcos was a "friend."[92] Such a response also resulted from his pro-American business policies, made clear only after the imposition of martial law. Referring to three Supreme Court decisions favoring the Nnationalists, which had caused great concern for American business, Marcos said he would clarify those decisions, "if necessary by decree."[93] Marcos repeatedly assured foreign businesses that there would be no nationalization. According to Marcos, those who owned land or managed businesses would be allowed to continue to do so even after the expiration of "parity rights."[94]

Finance Secretary Cesar Virata read a speech for Marcos before the Asia-Pacific Council of the American Chamber of Commerce in which the president said: "I want to reassure those concerned that this matter shall be pursued in the spirit of justice and fairness to all. . . . If expropriation is to be undertaken, just compensation will be forthcoming. We will be fair and just in all these matters."[95]

Estimating U.S. holdings in the Philippines at about $1 billion, Secretary Virata stated that only a "small portion" would be affected by the termination of "parity rights" in 1974.[96]

The president was more reassuring to American investors in an interview with *U.S. News & World Report* published on October 26, 1972. He said: "We're interested in all forms of foreign capital and I would like to emphasize two things: We will offer as much incentive as is possible and foreign capital will be protected. There will be no confiscation while I am president. Such things as amortization of investment, retirement of capital, and transmittal of profits are guaranteed."[97] The Americans adopted a "wait-and-see" policy and later gave more aid and support to the newly formed martial law government of Marcos.

Henry Byroade, American ambassador to the Philippines, had a long conference with Marcos before the imposition of martial law. Marcos likely informed the State Department of the imminent imposition of martial rule, in which the U.S. government saw no threat to its interests.[98] Whether the U.S. government was officially informed or consulted in the process, the fact remains that the U.S. government, including President Nixon and the State Department, neither registered disapproval nor made comment.

A U.S. Congress committee conducted research in the Philippines between November 2 and November 18, 1972, barely a month after Marcos took over. James Lowenstein and Richard M. Moose looked into the general situation in two Asian countries where martial law had just been imposed: South Korea and the Philippines. On January 17, 1973, they submitted their report to Senator Fulbright, chairman of the Senate Committee on Foreign Relations. In the report they described the situation in these countries as they "relate[d] to United States interests and programs."[99] Lowenstein and Moose reported on the political and economic conditions surrounding the declaration of emergency rule and examined related conditions in both countries. The report concluded, among other things, that the United States should assume greater responsibility in the region. It stated: We saw no evidence of any diminished sense of U.S. responsibility for either government.

Indeed, in so far as material aid is concerned, it would appear that in the coming year the Congress will be asked to do more for both countries."[100]

Regarding democratic practice and U.S. interest, the report made significant statements worth quoting at length:

We found few, if any, Americans who took the position that the demise of individual rights and democratic institutions would adversely affect U.S. interests. In the first place, these democratic institutions were considered to be severely deficient. In the second place, whatever U.S. interests were, or are, they apparently are not thought to be related to the preservation of democratic processes. Even in the Philippines, our own colonial stepchild and the "showcase of democracy" in Asia, the United States appears to have adopted a new pragmatism (perhaps because there was no other choice), turning away from evangelical hopes and assumptions with which it has tended to look at the political evolution. Thus, U.S. officials appear prepared to accept that the strengthening of presidential authority will . . . enable President Marcos to introduce needed stability; that this objective is in our interest; and . . . stability . . . and military bases and a familiar government in the Philippines, are more important than the preservation of democratic institutions which were imperfect at best."[101]

U.S. interest and the avowed policy of being the leading light of democracy and individual rights were shown to be unrelated to each other. The imposition of martial law in the Philippines put to test the democratic rhetoric of U.S. foreign policy.

On September 26, 1972, three days after the announcement of the imposition of martial law, Marcos outlined the contours of his economic policy to foreign journalists:

1. To permit those holdings, whose titles have been nullified by the Supreme Court, to be disposed of over a long period of time to individual Filipinos or to companies meeting the legal requirements of 60 per cent Filipino ownership.

2. To permit foreigners to act as directors or serve in executive management positions of certain kinds of companies that the Supreme Court [had] said could not employ aliens.

3. To interpret Philippine retail-trade law in a way that would permit the bulk sale of oil to industrial users.

4. To facilitate foreign exploration for oil in the Philippines by not requiring oil companies to obtain leases but instead allowing them to operate on service contracts with the government. Through operating contracts, the foreign companies would receive compensation similar to that obtained from leasing.[102]

To attract multinational corporations to establish their area or regional headquarters in the Philippines, Presidential Decree No. 218 (June 16, 1973) amended by Presidential Decree No. 348 (December 22, 1973) gave lucrative incentives.[103] Non-Filipino personnel of multinational corporations establishing their headquarters in the Philippines and their dependents were exempted from Philippine income tax, immigration and alien registration fees, customs duties on personal effects, and clearance requirements. Multinationals were also declared exempt from the 3% contractor's tax, license fees, and dues, and they also enjoyed free taxation from imported goods, including cars. Multiple entry visas valid for one year were to be issued to them to facilitate travel in and out of the country. To make the Philippines even more attractive to multinational corporations, Marcos also decreed that they could repatriate profits and be exempt from expropriation. Repatriation of all profits was allowed in the currency of the original investment, and those profits could be remitted at the current rate of exchange. Assurance against divestiture or expropriation by the government was given except in cases for public use, such as welfare and defense, and only upon payment of just compensation.[104]

By 1981 about 200 multinational company headquarters in the Philippines had organized themselves as the Philippine Association of Multinational Companies Regional Headquarters, Inc. (PAMURI). The association fully supported government efforts to attract more multinational firms to establish their headquarters in the Philippines.[105] An earlier ruling relaxed travel arrangements for investors: Land developers for tourism projects and investors coming to the Philippines for a minimum of seventy-two hours regardless of nationality could enter the Philippines without visas, whereas previously a visa had been required together with a posted bond.[106]

An important economic measure enacted immediately after the declaration of martial law was the stalled oil exploration bill in the Philippine Congress. Presidential Decree No. 8 issued on October 2, 1972, laid down the principles to attract foreign investors to oil exploration.[107] It was reported that Marcos told U.S. oil executives: "We'll pass the law you need. Just tell us what you want."[108] Presidential Decree No. 8 was further amended by Presidential Decree No. 87, issued on December 31, 1972. Those decrees were collectively known as "The Oil Exploration and Development Act of 1972." The act was again amended in May 23, 1974, by Presidential Decree No. 469. The oil exploration decrees allowed companies, even those owned owned by foreign nationals, to engage in oil exploration under service contracts with the Philippine government.[109] It was considered that the package of incentives offered by the Philippines was by far the most liberal and generous. It included tax concessions, cost recovery, and production-sharing benefits, where foreign companies would retain 40% of oil profits, after deducting costs, tax-free.[110] With such incentives, several companies—including Rockefeller Center, Inc., Westrans Petroleum, Champlin Philippines Industries, Standard Oil of California, and Sun Oil Industries—engaged in oil exploration in the Philippines.[111] Oil refiners, such as American-owned Caltex, Esso Eastern, Getty, and Gulf Oil were also allowed to sell in bulk to industrial users in spite of the prohibition that resulted from the interpretation of the retail-trade nationalization law with regard to end-users and bulk sales.[112] Incentives similar to the oil exploration decree were given to the mining industry. To induce business activity, the stock market trading transfer tax was reduced from 2% to 0.25 of 1%.[113]

To further attract foreign investors, Marcos enacted favorable labor and wage laws as incentives to investment. By virtue of General Order No. 5, strikes were banned. On May 1, Labor Day of 1974, Marcos decreed the Philippine Labor Code or the Magna Carta of Labor. In the pursuit of "industrial peace" and the encouragement of incentives to business, strikes were banned in "vital industries," reinforcing the earlier rule of General Order No. 5. That rule was also provided for in NEDA's Economic Development Plan of 1974-77. "Vital industries" was defined at the discretion of the Ministry of Labor and could therefore be subject to arbitrariness and wide interpretation.[114]

Wages in the Philippines were the lowest in Asia. Government policy kept salaries as low as possible in order to attract multinationals to establish plants in the Philippines. Marcos announced the policy on January 4, 1974, on the occasion of the Philippine Central Bank's Silver Anniversary celebration:

Our country now has one of the lowest average wage levels. . . . We intend to see to it that our export program is not placed in jeopardy at an early stage by a rapid rise in the general wage level. . . . We shall preserve the relative position of our wage structure vis-à-vis those of competing countries.[115]

If success in wage policy were measured in terms of maintenance or decrease in real wages, the Marcos administration was highly successful. The Central Bank report for 1980 stated that "real wages for skilled workers were 63.7% and for unskilled workers 53.4% of what they had been in 1972."[116]

In 1980, when the possibility of lifting martial law was indicated, multinational corporations expressed concern about the results. According to A. Lewis Burridge, president of Sterling Asia and a member of PAMURI, "MNC's [multinational corporations] believe martial law declared by President Marcos eight years ago had created 'favorable conditions for economic expansion.' "[117] Business people were worried that the lifting of martial law would hamper their operations and bring back the conditions of the late 1960s. They expressed their concerns in a meeting with the minister of trade, Luis Villafuerte; they asked for additional concessions and privileges, including the waiving of permits and fees to the Philippine International Trading Corporation (PITC) whenever its members traded with socialist countries.

With the imposition of martial law, Marcos started to open the way for a development policy heavily dependent on foreign capital and investment. He reversed the earlier policy of Congress and reversed Supreme Court decisions. His moves were facilitated by his free hand in policy making, the benefit of silenced critics, and a centralized decision-making process. Marcos had a bureaucracy and a group of technocrats to implement his instructions. With the stroke of a pen, several decrees were issued offering various incentives, tax breaks to foreign business ventures, and multinational corporations, as well as the exploitation and use of Philippine natural resources.

In the hope of producing another economic miracle in the Asia Pacific region, the Marcos regime copied the development model of its Asian neighbors: Singapore, Taiwan, and South Korea. On the assumption that capital was the main ingredient needed to reach the "takeoff" stage of development, all possible sources of capital were tapped. Marcos's policy also assumed that in order to attain rapid economic development, civil liberties should be restrained and that society needed to be depoliticized; however, restraining political and civil liberties contradicted the U.S. goal of promoting democracy and human rights.

In the course of legitimizing and institutionalizing authoritarianism in the Philippines, individual rights, electoral politics, and an open political system, often identified with what American democracy stood for, were set aside or violated. Pragmatism and U.S. interest prevailed over violated democratic ideals. In examining the major elements of U.S.-Philippine relations, the military bases in the Philippines, U.S. business and investment, and economic and military aid, a congressional committee concluded that "Marcos is highly dependent both upon U.S. investment and the aid to which bases are linked." In its dealings with the Philippines, the United States reckoned with its own commitments and interests while Marcos pursued his objectives with the United States "as patron and protector."[118]

In the economic and strategic fields, the United States found in the Marcos government a guarantor of its interests. American administrations may have expressed dismay over Marcos's human rights record, but by giving him aid, they supported the maintenance of his regime.

NOTES

1. Primitivo Mijares, *The Conjugal Dictatorship of Ferdinand and Imelda Marcos I*, (San Francisco: Union Square Publications, 1976) p. 140.

2. Ibid., pp. 134-135.

3. John H. Adkins, "Philippines 1972: We'll Wait and See," *Asian Survey* 21:1 (January 1972): 143. In the first week of 1972, Marcos retired "18 generals, 20 colonels, and 13 lieutenant colonels and reappointed Juan Ponce-Enrile, who was defeated senatorial candidate, as secretary of defense. From Reuben R. Canoy, *The Counterfeit Revolution: Martial Law in the Philippines* (Manila: Philippine Editions Publishing, 1980), p. 20; Carl H. Lande, "Philippine Prospects after Martial Law," *Foreign Affairs* 59 (1981): 1156.

4. John F. Doherty, "Who Controls the Philippine Economy: Some Need Not Try as Hard as Others" (Manoa: University of Hawaii, 1982), p. 30.

5. "Some Are Smarter than Others" (pamphlet was prepared by "a group of concerned businesspeople and professional managers," 1979).

6. Horacio Paredes, "Most Powerful Man outside Marcos," *Government Depth News Asia* (July 6, 1984); Philippine Resource Center, *Sourcebook on the Philippine Economic Crisis* (Berkeley: Philippine Resource Center, 1984), pp. 82ff.

7. Fred Poole and Max Vanzi, *Revolution in the Philippines: The United States in a Hall of Cracked Mirrors* (New York: McGraw-Hill Book Co., 1984), p. 254.

8. Ibid., p. 253.

9. Peter Carey, Katherine Ellinson, and Lewis M. Simons, "Hidden Billions: The Draining of the Philippines," *San Jose Mercury News*, June 23-25, 1985.

10. Paul Gigot, "Crony Capitalism Slaps Philippines," *Asian Wall Street Journal*, November 8, 1983, in Philippine Resource Center, *Sourcebook*, p. 80.

11. "Some Are Smarter than Others."

12. Gary Hawes, "The Growing Role of the State in the Philippines: Economic or Political Response to Capitalist Development?" (paper presented at the 1983 Meeting of the Association for Asian Studies, San Francisco, March 25-27), p. 21.

13. Gigot, "Crony Capitalism."

14. Jose V. Abueva, "The Philippines: Tradition and Change," *Asian Survey* 10:1 (January 1970): 63.

15. *New York Times*, December 19, 1969, p. 41.

16. Robert O. Tilman, "The Philippines in 1970: A Difficult Decade Begins," *Asian Survey* (January 1971): 140.

17. Abueva, "The Philippines," p. 62.

18. Ibid.

19. *Far Eastern Economic Review*, September 14, 1989, pp. 36ff.

20. Norman G. Owen, ed., *Compadre Colonialism: Studies on the Philippines under American Rule* (Ann Arbor: University of Michigan Center for South and Southeast Asian Studies, 1975).

21. The story of the presidency of Magsaysay illustrates this. See Jose V. Abueva, *Ramon Magsaysay: A Political Biography* (Manila: Solidaridad Publishing House, 1971).

22. Claude A. Buss, *The United States and the Philippines: Background for Policy* (Washington, DC: American Enterprise Institute for Public Policy Research; and Stanford: Hoover Institute on War, Revolution and Peace, 1977), p. 46.

23. Quoted in Teodoro A. Agoncillo and Oscar M. Alfonso, *History of the Filipino People* (Quezon City: Malaya Books, 1967), p. 574.

24. *Symington Hearings*, p. 356.

25. U.S. Department of State, *Bulletin*, October 10, 1966, p. 529.

26. Marcos's speech before the U.S. Congress, *Congressional Record*, September 15, p. 21818; also in U.S. Department of State *Bulletin*, p. 537-547.

27. Ibid., p. 542.

28. Ibid.

29. Ibid., p. 547.

30. Ibid., p. 533.

31. "Joint Communique," in ibid.

32. *New York Times*, October 28, 1966, p. 2.

33. Ibid.

34. Buss, *The United States and the Philippines*, p. 51.

35. *New York Times*, October 25, 1966, p. 1.

36. Symington Hearings.

37. Ibid., pp. 254-255.

38. *New York Times*, January 1, 1970, p. 4.

39. Symington Hearings, p. 287.

40. Ibid., p. 61.

41. Ibid., p. 263.

42. Ibid., p. 262.

43. Ibid., p. 273.

44. *New York Times*, March 16, 1970, p. 16.

45. Ibid., March 20, 1970, p. 2.

46. Ibid., March 26, 1970, p. 9.

47. Ibid.

48. Ibid.

49. Ibid., March 27, 1970, p. 5.

50. Ibid., March 31, 1970, p. 8.

51. Ibid., April 1, 1970, p. 4.

52. U.S. Congress, Senate, Committee on Foreign Relations, *Korea and the Philippines: November 1972*, 93rd Cong., 1st sess., 1973, p. 47.

53. Larry A. Niksch and Marjorie Niehaus, *The Internal Situation in the Philippines; Current Trends and Future Prospects* (Washington, DC: Congressional Research Service, Library of Congress, January 20, 1981), pp. 129-134.

54. Ibid.

55. International Ecumenical Conference on the Philippines, "Cry of the People, Challenge to the Churches: A Report of the International Ecumenical Conference on the Philippines" (Stony Point, New York, October 2, 1983).

56. Richard J. Kessler, "Marcos and the Americans," *Foreign Policy* 63 (summer 1986): 44.

57. Sudershan Chawla et al., *Changing Patterns of Security and Stability in Asia* (New York: Praeger Publishers, 1980), p. 72. Also see "The Nixon Doctrine," February 1971, and President Nixon's Guam doctrine, July 1969, in the appendices of Chawla.

58. Alvin J. Cottrell and Robert J. Hanks, *The Military Utility of the U.S. Facilities in the Philippines* (Washington, DC: Georgetown University, Center for Strategic and International Studies, 1980), p. 5.

59. U.S. Congress, House, Committee on Foreign Affairs, *United States-Philippine Relations and the New Base and Aid Agreement: Hearings before the Subcommittee on Asian and Pacific Affairs*, statement of Adm. Robert J. Long, U.S. Navy, Commander-in-Chief, Pacific, 98th cong., 1st sess., 1983 p. 38.

60. Roland G. Simbulan, *Our Bases of Insecurity: A Study of U.S. Military Bases in the Philippines* (Manila: BALAI Fellowship, 1983), p. 116.

61. Jeanne Kirkpatrick, "Dictatorships and Double Standards," *Commentary* 68:5 (November 1979): 34-45; and David Forsythe, *Human Rights and World Politics* (Lincoln: University of Nebraska Press, 1983), pp. 92-93.

62. S. R. Shalom, *The United States and the Philippines: A Study of Neocolonialism* (Philadelphia: Institute for the Study of Human Issues, 1981), p. 181.

63. Forsythe, *Human Rights and World Politics*, pp. 96-97.

64. Jim Morrell, "Aid to the Philippines: Who Benefits?" *International Policy Report* 5:2 (October 1979): p. 3.

65. Quoted in Barry Rubin, "The Reagan Administration and the Middle East," in Kenneth A. Oye et al., *Eagle Defiant: United States Foreign Policy in the 1980s* (Boston: Little, Brown, and Co., 1983), p. 373.

66. Assistant Secretary Richard Holbrooke's testimony before the hearings of the House of Representatives, Committee on Asian and Pacific Affairs, February 21, 1979.

67. Kenneth A. Oye, "International Systems Structure and American Foreign Policy," in Oye et al., *Eagle Defiant*, pp. 3ff.

68. "The States-Item," *Times-Picayune* (New Orleans), September 18, 1982, in *Editorials on File* 13:18 (September 16-30, 1982): 1106.

69. Ibid.

70. Jovito R. Salonga, "The New Bases Agreement: An Analysis and a Suggestion," in Bishops-Businessmen's Conference, *Not by Bread Alone: Dialogue on Human Development under Martial Law* (Manila, 1980), pp. 140-161.

71. Art. XIII, Sect. 1, the 1935 Philippine Constitution; see Zaide, *Philippine Government,* pp. 295-296.

72. Ibid., pp. 295-296.

73. Agoncillo and Alfonso, *History*, p. 508.

74. Quoted in Shalom, *The United States*, p. 57.

75. Ibid., pp. 57-58.

76. Civil Case No. 10732, Court of First Instance, Rizal, Seventh Judicial District, Branch XIII (1969), quoted in Alejandro M. Fernandez, *The Philippines and the United States: The Forging of New Relations* (Quezon City: NSDB-UP Integrated Research Program, 1977) pp. 404-405. Vested interest rights theory refers to the "rights that are vested when the enjoyment, present or prospective, has become the property of some particular persons or persons as a particular interest," Fernandez, ibid., p. 468.

77. Ibid., in *Republic of the Philippines and/or Solicitor General v. William H. Quasha*, G.R. No. L-30299, August 17, 1972.

78. *New York Times*, August 25, 1972, p. 31.

79. Robert B. Stauffer, "Political Economy of Refeudalization," in David A. Rosenberg, ed., *Marcos and Martial Law in the Philippines* (Ithaca, NY: Cornell University Press, 1979), p. 188.

80. Agoncillo and Alfonso, *History*, p. 610; Remigio E. Agpalo, *The Political Process and the Nationalization of the Retail Trade in the Philippines* (Quezon City: University of the Philippines Press, 1962).

81. Fernandez, *The Philippines and the U.S.*, p. 408.

82. Ibid.

83. White House press release dated October 6, 1964, in Department of State, *Bulletin* 51:1323 (November 2, 1964): 632-534.

84. Agoncillo and Alfonso, *History*, p. 610.

85. Fernandez, *The Philippines and the U.S.*, p. 409.

86. *New York Times*, December 23, 1966, p. 9.

87. Agoncillo and Alfonso, *History,* p. 610.

88. *New York Times*, January 27, 1967, p. 63.

89. *Philippine News*, November 21-27, 1984, p. 1.

90. *Time*, October 9, 1972, p. 27.

91. Quoted in Walden Bello and Elaine Elinson, *Elite Democracy or Authoritarian Rule*. (Manila: Nationalist Resource Center, 1981), p. 8.

92. *New York Times* (Business and Finance), November 1972, p. 53.

93. Ibid.

94. Ibid., October 4, 1972, p. 14.

95. *Wall Street Journal*, October 24, 1972, p. 15.

96. Ibid.

97. Alejandro M. Fernandez, "The Philippines and the United States Today," in *Southeast Asian Affairs 1976* (Singapore: Institute of Southeast Asian Studies, 1977), p. 292.

98. Poole and Vanzi, *Revolution in the Philippines*, U.S. Congress, Senate, Committee on Foreign Relations, p. 269.

99. *Korea and the Philippines*, vii.

100. Ibid., p. 45.

101. Ibid.

102. *New York Times*, February 15, 1973.

103. Ibid., April 1973, p. 13.

104. The following discussion and quotations were based on the Supreme Court decision *Javellana v. Executive Secretary et al.* L-36142, and most specifically on the resume of Chief Justice Roberto Concepcion.

105. Quoted in *New York Times*, April 1973, p. 13.

106. Ibid.

107. Ibid., February 15, 1973, p. 6.

108. Ibid.

109. Marcos, *Democratic Revolution*, p. 183.

110. *New York Times*, April 1973, p. 8.

111. Marcos, *Democratic Revolution*, p. 188.

112. *New York Times*, January 18, 1973, p. 8.

113. Ibid.

114. Niksch and Niehaus, *International Situation in the Philippines*, p. 10.

115. *New York Times*, August 1, 1973, p. 5.

116. Jovito R. Salonga, Horacio de la Costa et al., *A Message of Hope to Filipinos Who Care: Containing an Analysis of Three Years of Martial Law, an Evaluation of the New Society* (Manila: October 1, 1975), p. 20.

117. William Butler, John Humphrey, and G. E. Bisson, *The Decline of Democracy in the Philippines* (Geneva: International Commission of Jurists, 1977), pp. 62-63.

118. *U.S. Congress Korea and the Philippines*, p. 47.

Chapter 6

Decline and Fall of the Dictatorship

The attempt at total control does not merely corrupt, as Acton said, it debilitates.
It undoes itself.[1]

On August 21, 1983, Benigno Aquino, Marcos's chief political rival, was gunned down at Manila International Airport. After three years in the United States, he returned to his native country to lead the opposition and save the Philippines from political chaos and economic ruin resulting from Marcos's misrule. Deteriorating economic conditions, aggravated by power struggles fanned by rumors of Marcos's ill health, and the Aquino assassination triggered massive public protests. Aquino's death showed the vulnerability of even one of the most prominent families in the country under the regime. Daily demonstrations, rallies, and protests were held, especially in Makati, the financial capital and bastion of wealth in the Philippines.

Marcos scheduled an early presidential election in January 1986 to prove that he still had the support of the people. The opposition remained fractious about its official nominee, but at the last minute Cardinal Jaime Sin forged a compromise. Salvador Laurel agreed to be the vice-presidential candidate to allow Corazon Aquino to lead the opposition ticket. Benigno's widow attracted widespread support from various social and economic sectors. She aroused public sympathy and the hope of removing the ailing dictator. Business and economic elites openly campaigned for her because of their dissatisfaction with economic performance under Marcos. Aquino's mass following, however, did not translate to electoral victory because Marcos controlled the balloting, reporting, and tallying process. After Marcos was finally ousted, the military admitted to committing fraud and using intimidation. Its leader, Secretary of Defense Juan Ponce-Enrile, admitted to stuffing the ballot boxes for Marcos in his home region, Cagayan. Blatant fraud was also documented by international media and official observers from the United States. In protest, Aquino claimed victory and led demonstrations to protest Marcos's claims. What immediately caused Marcos's ouster, however, was the revolt of the military reform leaders in February 1986. The rebel soldiers and officers who barricaded themselves in the armed forces headquarters were eventually joined by other elements of society in response to the radio message of Cardinal Sin, the archbishop of Manila. The revolt, called the "People Power Revolution," was confined to metropolitan Manila, specifically along a strip of the main thoroughfare surrounding the armed forces headquarters at EDSA (Epifanio de los Santos Avenue), close to shopping centers, government offices, posh neighborhoods, and other symbols of modernity and privilege. In addition to the military, revolt leaders were from the clergy, business, academia, government offices, and the opposition, that is, largely from the traditional political sector. Leftist and communists did not participate as a group. The rural populace was not immediately affected by the four-day rebellion that took place in front of television cameras broadcast all over the world. Television viewers in the United States were fed minute-by-minute coverage of the fall of the Marcos dictatorship and saw more of it than millions of people in the rural Philippines. At the invitation of the Reagan administration, Marcos fled the Philippines via U.S.-provided transport to exile in Hawaii. Career foreign service and defense officials finally persuaded and prevailed upon Marcos's loyal ally, President Ronald Reagan, to withdraw its support from the continuance of Marcos's rule and paved the way for the transfer of power to Aquino. Marcos left the Philippines with democracy in shambles and its economy in ruins.

PROMISE OF A NEW SOCIETY

"Sa ikauunlad ng bayan, disiplina ang kailangan" ("Discipline is a requirement of national development") was the slogan of Marcos's New Society: the Philippines under martial law. Through a constitutionally authoritarian government, Marcos promised a developed society. He asserted that in fact martial law "together with the New Society that has emerged from its reforms . . . a revolution of the poor . . . is aimed at protecting the individual, helpless until then, from the power of the oligarchs."[2]

If the promises for political order and economic development were the legal bases of Marcos's rule, he was unable to fulfill his mandate or to conform to the principles behind his claim to legitimacy. Behind the appearance of the stability of the authoritarian system was its weakness: growing insurgency, economic decline, and dissension. The undercurrent of weakness in the regime was seen in the disparity between its promise in 1972 and its performance after the state of emergency was lifted. The insurgency movement that was the primary impetus for martial law gained more supporters. The NPA guerrillas, estimated at between 10,000 to 15,000 in 1985, were operating in all parts of the Philippines. The National Democratic Front (NDF), the coalition behind the NPA, claimed the mass base support of 10 million.[3] The country experienced rapid decline in its productivity and living standards. Poverty was widespread, more than 60% lived below the poverty level. Real wages declined and unemployment and underemployment increased.

Statistics record Marcos's legacy. In 1984, the United States Agency for International Development (USAID) estimated that at least 39% of the population lived below the poverty level, whereas in a 1980 report, the World Bank placed it at 42%.[4] Sixty percent of urban families fell below that level. Other studies estimated that as much as 64% of the Philippine population lived below the poverty level. Between 1960 and 1980, the economy experienced an average annual growth of 2.8%. The Marcos government claimed credit for the growth rate (6.5%) in the GNP during the 1970s.[5] The GNP, the commonly accepted measure of economic development, declined to 4.7% in 1980, 3.6% in 1981, 2.8% in 1982, 1.41% in 1983, and 6% in 1984.[6]

The decline in the early 1980s resulted from several factors. Even when there was growth, lopsided income distribution ironically persisted if not worsened. The USAID studies stated that "growth in the Philippines has tended to reinforce uneven income distribution. The lowest 20% of households still receives less than 6% of the income and the highest 20% receives over 53%."[7] Comparative data can be gleaned from estimates based on the National Census and Statistics Office (NCSO) of the Philippine government's integrated survey of households in 1971 and 1979:

The poorest 60% of total households, which received only 25% of total income in 1971, suffered a further decline of their share to 22.5% in 1979 while the richest 10% of households increased their share of total income from 37.1% in 1971 to 41.7% in 1979.[8]

Since 1972, there had been a nominal increase in wages. According to the Central Bank of the Philippines however, there was a steep decline in real terms. There was an increase of 174.7% and 155.5% for salaried workers and wage earners respectively. After eight years, the salaried workers' real wages were 93.2% and for regular wage earners 86.7% of the 1972 base. In 1980 Manila's skilled laborers' earnings were only 63.7% of the 1972 level, while the unskilled laborers suffered a decrease to 53.4%.[9] The country's minimum-wage laws favored industrial over agricultural workers, further contributing to rural-urban disparities. Based on various studies summarized in Tables 1 and 2, the legislated minimum wage was not enough to cross even the poverty threshold.[10]

An average Filipino needed to earn 50% more income to live on subsistence level, Based on estimates by the NEDA (National Economic Development Authority), the Philippine government's planning body and a private think-tank Center for Research and Communication (CRC).[11]

Table 1
Legislated Minimum Wages, Poverty Thresholds, and Indigency Income Levels, February 1984

A. Legislated Basic Minimum Wage and Supplements-National Wage
   Council (December 31, 1983)
   1. Non-Agricultural
      a. National Capital Region - P42.07/day; P1,062.27/mo.(a)
      b. Outside Natl.Capital Region - P40.99/day; 869.10(a)
   2. Agricultural
      a. Plantation - P34.42/day; P869.10/mo.(a)
      b. Non-plantation - P25.90/day; P653.98/mo.(a)
B. Poverty Threshold
   1. Abrera(1974): 6 member household
      Manila & suburb - P2997.85/mo.

Table 1 (continued)

          Other urban areas - P2,487.76/mo.
          Rural - P2,171.74
2.   Center for Research & Communication
          January 1982: 5-member household
          Threshold family income - Metro Manila - P3,515.12/mo.
3.   Tan-Holazo(1975): With food variety; 6-member household
          Metro Manila - P1,306.36
          Philippines - P1,082.43
4.   World Bank (1975): 6-member household - "least cost"
          consumption basket
          Urban - P3,469.92/mo.
          Rural - P2,613.12/mo.
          Philippines - P2,784.48/mo.

C. Indigency Income (July 7, 1982): Ministry of Social Services & Development (b)
    1.   Urban: 6-member household or less - P400/mo.; more than 6-member household - P450/mo.
    2.   Rural: 6-member household or less - P350/mo.; more than 6-member household - P400/mo.
        a. As of December 31, 1983 to April 30, 1984; daily wage multiplied by 25.25 days per month (NWC formula)
        b. MSSD Administrative Order No. 115, Series of 1982.

Table 2
Cost of Living vs. Monthly Wage

Source	Basic Needs/Month	Income: (Income as % of Needs)	Deficit (Addtl. Income as % of Needs)
NEDA(a)	P2, 571.00	P1, 557.60 (60.58%)	P1,013.40 (39.41%)
CRC(b)	P3, 940.00	P1, 557.60 (39.53%)	P1, 013.40 (63.00%)

    The Philippine government itself was short of money to fund its operations and had been operating on deficit spending. Between 1979 and 1981, the government's average annual total revenue was $4.562 billion whereas its expenditures were approximately $5.05 billion. In 1981 alone its deficit was approximately $1.264 billion or at least 22%.[12]

    Rapid inflation pinched Filipino consumers. Beginning in 1972, prices of commodities rose rapidly. In 1980 inflation was 10%; by 1984 it was estimated at 20% to 30%.[13]

    Unemployment and underemployment were high. For those earning regular incomes, meeting basic needs was difficult. For those not earning regular incomes, meeting those needs was impossible. It was conservatively estimated that unemployment and underemployment in the Philippines in 1985 was 30%. In the beginning of the 1980s it was 20%.[14] An unusually high growth rate of the labor supply and the labor force resulted from an increase in population as well as from the swelling of the ranks of households needing more income and employment to supplement meager resources. Using the basic-needs approach and the corresponding indicators, one may glean the level of development from Table 3.[15]

Malnutrition was prevalent throughout the Philippines, and by 1977 it placed third as a cause of death; in 1973 it was seventh. The most prevalent causes of death were pneumonia, gastroenteritis, and tuberculosis. The number of underweight and malnourished children climbed from 69% in 1965 to 80% in 1982. Some cases were severe enough to cause permanent brain damage or death. Malnutrition and its negative consequences to health and well-being were shared by the young, who comprised the predominant segment of the population. There were only thirty-six doctors per 100,000 persons, and most of the doctors were in urban areas. Sixty percent of deaths occurred without medical attention.[16]

Table 3
Basic Needs and Indicators of Development

Basic Needs	Indicators
Health	Life expectancy at birth - 62.2 years
Education	Literacy (10 years and above) - 89% Primary school enrollment as to the percentage of the population aged five to fourteen - Not available
Food	Calorie supply per head or calorie supply as a percentage of requirements - 84% of recommended minimum daily allowance (average caloric intake) Infant mortality per thousand births - 60.6 (Most developed nations have below 25% per thousand live births)
Water supply	Percentage of the population with access to potable water - 47%
Sanitation	Percentage of the population with access to sanitation facilities - Not available

The Philippine national economy was also marked by dependency on the international market and its economic forces. The prices of the islands' major exports—copra, sugar, and wood—are vulnerable to fluctuations in the international market.[17]

The Philippines imported 93% of its energy requirements mostly in the form of oil from the Middle East. Importing oil perennially aggravated the balance of payments. According to the *Far Eastern Economic Review*, between 1977 and 1981 the average negative balance of payments was minus -$265.6 million.[18] In another collection of statistics, the negative balance of payments was estimated as minus $86 million in 1978 and $2.1 billion in 1983. The balance-of-trade deficit worsened from $1.3 billion in 1978 to $2.4 billion in 1983.[19] The balance-of-trade deficit of $2 billion in 1980 was more than the total balance-of-trade deficit between 1960 and 1974.[20]

Foreign debt increased from $2.66 billion in 1972 to approximately $26 billion in 1984.[21] In 1983 the Philippines was unable to pay its loans. As a result, the IMF imposed greater fiscal austerity and budgetary and monetary control measures. It also required an increase of taxation and a devaluation in the rescheduling negotiations and agreements.[22]

In an economy of scarcity, where very few can enjoy a comfortable income or can control the resources, dependencies are reinforced. Opportunities are in the hands of the few. Their hold on the economy vis-à-vis the majority means influence and power; thus, dependency is not only a domestic phenomenon. It is also a national predicament.

The economic troubles bankrupted the bureaucracy. Scarcity of money reached a point where bureaucrats could no longer afford the reward system or the maintenance of the patron-client network. The massive outflow of government funds and resources for image-building projects, for graft and corruption, for rescuing cronies from failing businesses, for overinvolvement in capital investments and in the private sector, and for financing bribes for elections and referendums tremendously strained the public coffers. The disparities between those who were "in" government, the "haves," compared to those who were "out" of government, the "have nots," contributed to the perception of a regime of repression. The Filipino people saw that Marcos had already lost the authority to govern.

The scope of government expanded through increased personnel, offices, and operations. It permeated the private sector by granting tax exemptions, loan guarantees, privileges, and monopolies to key industries and products to selected businesspeople. It engaged in deficit spending and consequently incurred more debts in order to sustain massive operations such as investment and capitalization, business takeovers and assumption of loans and obligations, and infrastructure building. Such government involvement resulted in the concentration of wealth and the control of business through a network of a few families who were all related to the Marcoses and their close friends. The regime also had access to that network.

Before 1972 the "division of the pie" was established through elections. Positions of authority changed hands in a game with set rules, played by the elite: biennial elections with predictable results. Through those elections, the winners get the rewards and the losers wait for the next election to get their share. Parties were not ideologically different. They were only alliances of those who were "in" or those who were "out." When he imposed martial law in 1972, Marcos changed the rules by which politics was played. The "division of the pie" was decided through government expansion from which the spoils to be distributed came in the form of monopolies, contracts, projects, and other favors. Marcos centralized the patron-client network into one structure by fusing the executive and legislative branches and the bureaucracy into one unit and by expanding their resources and strengthening their powers.

LEGACY OF AUTHORITARIANISM

Marcos left a bureaucracy of pervasive influence and power. He increased bureaucratic intrusion into private relations and transactions. The locus of power of Philippine politics under Marcos was the civilian and the military bureaucracy. The process of governance was focused on the bureaucracy. Other branches of government such as the courts and legislative bodies, as well as other political entities, such as parties and interest groups, were subordinated and weakened by a powerful bureaucracy from which the authoritarian leader claimed his support. In the Philippine case, the network of alliances of the civilian and military bureaucracy was tied to patron-client relations and extended further to local politicians, business associates, and beneficiaries of the authoritarian system.

Standards of civil service eroded, and the abuse of public office became pervasive. Public bureaucracy was used for private gains such as the establishment of monopolies and the use of the public treasury for private wants and personal functions. Public officials blurred the boundaries between public and private domain. They overextended bureaucratic resources and time for patronage and image-building projects, thus increasing public spending and debt.

The military increased its power and influence and became more involved in politics. Civilian control over the military decreased as soldiers became involved in influencing the balance of power and influencing succession to power. Military professionalism was sacrificed in favor of loyalty and the democratic principle of civilian supremacy. The potential for instability increased because of the growing role of the armed forces. Threats of a military coup could destabilize and completely take over any government.

The lack of an orderly process for changing regimes and for transferring power, and the absence of predictability and stability in institutions and government practices weakened the constitution as a framework for political processes. While in power, Marcos based public policy on expediency and his needs to legitimize his power, preventing the participation of a greater number of citizens and the formulating of rational public policy. Marcos founded his government on a patron-client system, so the depletion of rewards endangered the foundation of the government. The breakup of such a system could in turn endanger those clients clinging to their privileges. Economic recovery is predicated on political stability, and political stability is predicated on a predictable system of succession of power. The threat of authoritarians using Marcos's justifications and tactics could disrupt stability and thus economic recovery and development. Marcos established the precedent for setting aside democratic processes.

NOTES

1. Gary Wills, *The Kennedy Imprisonment: A Meditation on Power*, (Boston: Little, Brown, and Co., 1981), p. 203.

2. Ferdinand E. Marcos, *The Democratic Revolution in the Philippines*, (Englewood Cliffs, New Jersey: Prentice Hall International, 1979), p. 1.

3. Permanent People's Tribunal Session on the Philippines, *Philippines: Repression and Resistance*, (London: Komite ng Sambayanang Pilipino, 1981), p. 203.

4. United States Agency for International Development (USAID: 1984), Taken from presentation reports to U.S. Congress, 1969-1984. Provided to the author in photocopies by the USAID Office at the U.S. Department of State.

5. Gerald Sussman, David O'Connor and Charles Lindsey, "Philippines, 1984: The Political Economy of a Dying Dictatorship," *Philippine Information Bulletin* (summer 1984) Philippine Information and Research Center, p. 3.

6. Ibid.

7. USAID (1983), p. 116.

8. Dante B. Canlas, et al. *An Analysis of the Philippine Economic Crisis: A Workshop Report*, (Quezon City: University of the Philippines School of Economics: June 1984), p. 36.

9. Ibid.

10. Ibid., p. 44.

11. Adapted from Joel Rocamora, "The Marcos Dictatorship, the IMF and the Philippine Economic Crisis," in *Sourcebook on the Philippine Economic Crisis: Analysis and Clippings* (Berkeley: Philippine Resource, Center [1985]), p. 2B.

12. Far Eastern Economic Review, *Asia Yearbook 1982*.

13. Joel Rocamora, "Testimonies on Economic Repression: US Imperialism and the Economic Crisis of Marcos Dictatorship," in *Philippines: Repression and Resistance*. Permanent People's Tribunal Session on the Philippines. (London: Komite ng Sambayanang Pilipino, 1980), pp. 73-74.

14. Canlas, *Analysis*, pp.44ff.

15. CHRP, *Fact Sheet*; the development indicators are from Paul Streeten, et al., *First Things First: Meeting Basic Human Needs in Developing Countries* (New York: Published for the World Bank by Oxford University Press, 1981).

16. CHRP, *Fact Sheet*.

17. Copra and sugar, the Philippines' main exports were placed under monopolies through Marcos's presidential decrees. Canlas, *Analysis*, see "3.1.3 Government Mandated Monopolies" and Paul A.Gigot, "Crony Capitalism Slaps Philippines," *Asian Wall Street Journal*, November 1983; and, Jonathan Kwitny, *Endless Enemies: The Making of an Unfriendly World* (New York: Congdon and Weed, Inc., 1984), Chapter 18.

18. Far Eastern Economic Review, *Ibid*.

19. Rocamora, "The Marcos Dictatorship," p.4A.

20. Rocamora, "Testimonies," pp. 73-74.

21. Rocamora, "The Marcos Dictatorship," p. 10A.

22. Articles of Andy McCue in the *Asian Wall Street Journal Weekly*, October and November 1983; Randolf David, "The Crisis: Allocation of its Burdens," *WHO Magazine* (Manila), July 18 and 25, 1984; and, Randolf David, "The IMF-Marcos Economic Adjustment Program: A Prescription for National Suicide," *WHO Magazine*, June 13, 1984.

Epilogue: The Philippines, 1986–1996

"Ang hindi marunong lumingon sa pinanggalingan ay hindi makakarating sa
paroroonan." (One who does not heed history will not see the future.)
—Tagalog Proverb

Nineteen ninety-six is a year of commemoration. It is the tenth year of the post-
Marcos era, the fiftieth year since Philippine independence from the United States,
and the one-hundredth year since the beginning of the 1896 Philippine revolution
against Spanish rule. The Philippine government inaugurated centennial celebrations
in 1996 culminating in the first one hundred years of the Republic (1998) with public
events and with scholars and historians gathered to examine the country's past.

Among the milestones of the country's modern history, Marcos's imposing of
martial law in 1972 remains a legacy. The ghost of Marcos will forever haunt the
Philippine political system. After his overthrow and exile to Hawaii, he plotted his
return to reclaim the seat of the presidency as rightfully his. Six coup-attempts
threatened his successor, Corazon Aquino. They were staged by factions of the
military, impatient with democratic reforms and messianic in their perception of
themselves as saviors of the country. Since Marcos's martial law, the Philippine
military has become a force to reckon with by the elected government and the
civilian bureaucracy.

The search for and attempt to recover Marcos's plunder, as well as that of his
cronies, has occupied the attention of the successor governments. The adjudication
of claims and the return of property to its rightful owners is fraught with
controversy. The pleas for justice from those whose rights were violated by the
martial-law regime continue to this day. The scars of torture, unresolved
"disappearances," and extra-judicial executions remain. Succeeding governments,
however, seem resolved that people's rights will be defended and that the systematic
looting of the national patrimony and abuses of power of the Marcos era will not be
allowed again.

Succeeding Marcos was indeed difficult in the aftermath of his misrule.
Expectations for President Corazon Aquino were high, while her supporters and

opponents were pulling at her administration from many directions. Her crowning achievements are the unification of forces against Marcos, which led to the return to a democratic constitution, and her steadfastness in times when democracy was in question.

General Fidel Ramos, a cousin of Ferdinand Marcos and one of his assistants, was elected by the Filipinos in 1992, in a multi-candidate race which included Imelda Marcos as a contender. Imelda continued to be in the public eye as she struggled to return Marcos's body for his final burial in the Philippines after his death in the U.S. in 1989. Even through her best source of influence, money, Imelda failed in her attempts to regain power. She has maintained a reputation for lavish spending from a bottomless source and for theatrical political shows.

As the second post-Marcos president, Ramos chose economic development as the primary goal of his tenure. "Philippines 2000" is a plan to catch up with the newly industrializing countries of Asia based on increased industry, developed technology and trade, and foreign investment. U.S. military installations, which were dismantled in 1992, have been targeted as growth centers for technology and commerce. While Ramos has remained committed to the constitution, issues relating to his tenure in office hover around him. There is a sense of satisfaction with his performance as economic indicators now turn from negative to positive. Because of economic improvements, political allies would like to revise the constitutional provisions about the term of office of the president. The post-Marcos constitution provided for a six-year term without re-election, a provision designed to prevent would-be authoritarians. The idea of shifting to a parliamentary form of government has also been floated. In the 1970s, a parliamentary government would have allowed President Ramos to serve as prime minister and to continue ruling the country. As was the Marcos maneuver in the 1970s, the main justification for the proposal is the attempt to find a political solution to achieving economic development. A sympathizer of an authoritarian system and a critic of democratic constitutions is Singapore's Senior Minister Lee Kuan Yew. He thinks that the failure of the Philippines political and economic system results from its democratic form. In looking back, one sees that the Philippines has tried both forms. One can clearly see and evaluate the results.

The period from 1972 to 1986, the period of Marcos's absolute rule, has left a cautionary lesson of the disastrous attempt of one man to dominate the political process in a populous country. Identification of historical guideposts serves the needs of the present as well as of the future. 1996 will be celebrated in the future not only as the centennial of the revolution but also as the beginning of democracy.

Selected Bibliography

BOOKS AND ARTICLES

Agoncillo, Teodoro A. and Alfonso, Oscar M. *History of the Filipino People*. Quezon City: Malaya Books, 1967.

Amnesty International. *Amnesty International Reports*. London, 1974, 1975, 1976, 1978, 1980.

_____. *Human Rights Violations in the Philippines: An Account of Torture, "Disappearances," Extrajudicial Executions and Illegal Detention*. London: Amnesty International, [1982?].

Aquino, Benigno S. "What's Wrong With the Philippines?" *Foreign Affairs* 46:4 (July 1968): 770-779.

Bello, Walden; Kinley, David; and Elinson, Elaine. *Development Debacle: The World Bank in the Philippines*. San Francisco: Institute for Food and Development Policy—Philippine Solidarity Network, 1982.

Bunge, Frederica, ed. *Philippines: A Country Study*. Washington D.C.: Foreign Area Studies, American University, 1983.

Buss, Claude A. *The United States and the Philippines: Background for Policy*. Washington D.C.: American Enterprise Institute for Public Policy Research and Stanford: Hoover Institute on War, Revolution and Peace, 1977.

Butler, William; Humphrey, John; and Bisson, G.E. *The Decline of Democracy in the Philippines*. Geneva: International Commission of Jurists, 1977.

Canlas, Dante B.; et al. *An Analysis of the Philippine Economic Crisis: A Workshop Report*. Quezon City: University of the Philippines School of Economics, June 1984.

Canoy, Reuben R. *The Counterfeit Revolution: Martial Law in the Philippines*. Manila: Philippine Editions Publishing, 1980.

Carey, Peter; Ellison, Katherine; Simons, Lewis M. "Hidden Billions: The Draining of the Philippines." *San Jose Mercury News*, June 23-25, 1985.

Constantino, Renato. *The Philippines: A Past Revisited*. Quezon City: Tala Publishing Services, 1975.

Constantino, Renato, and Constantino, Letizia R. *The Philippines: The Continuing Past*. Quezon City: Foundation for Nationalist Studies, 1978.

Corpuz, Onofre D. *Bureaucracy in the Philippines*. Manila: University of the Philippines, Institute of Public Administration, 1957.

_____. *The Philippines*. Englewood Cliffs, New Jersey: Prentice Hall, Inc., 1965.

Day, Beth Feagles. *The Philippines: Shattered Showcase of Democracy in Asia*. New York: M. Evans, 1974.

De Guzman, Raul P. "The Evolution of Filipino Political Institutions: Prospects for Normalization," *Philippine Journal of Public Administration* 26: 3&4 (July-October 1982): 205-218.

Diokno, Jose W. *Justice Under Siege: Five Talks*. Manila: Nationalist Resource Center, 1981.

Fernandez, Alejandro M. *The Philippines and the United States: The Forging of New Relations*. Quezon City: NSDB-Integrated Research Program, 1977.

Grossholtz, Jean. *Politics in the Philippines*. Boston: Little, Brown, and Company, 1964.

Hernandez, Carolina G. "The Extent of Civilian Control of the Military in the Philippines: 1946-1976." Ph.D. dissertation, State University of New York at Buffalo, 1979.

Huntington, Samuel P. *Political Order in Changing Societies*. New Haven, Conn.: Yale University Press, 1968.

Kessler, Richard. "The Philippines: The Next Iran?" *Asian Affairs. An American Review* 7:3 (January - February 1980): 148-160.

Kirkpatrick, Jeanne. "Dictatorships and Double Standards." *Commentary* 68:5 (November 1979): 34-45.

Klitgaard, Robert E. *Martial Law in the Philippines*. Santa Monica: Rand Corporation, 1972.

Kwitny, Jonathan. *Endless Enemies: The Making of an Unfriendly World*. New York: Congdon and Weed, Inc., 1984.

Lande, Carl H. "Authoritarian Rule in the Philippines: Some Critical Views." *Pacific Affairs* 55:1 (Spring 1982): 80-93.

The Lawyers Committee for International Human Rights. *The Philippines: A Country in Crisis*. New York: The Lawyers Committee for International Human Rights, 1983.

Liberal Party of the Philippines. *Vision and Program of Government*. Manila, 1985.

Marcos, Ferdinand E. *The Democratic Revolution in the Philippines*. 2nd ed. Englewood Cliffs, New Jersey: Prentice Hall International, 1979.

_____. *The New Philippine Republic: A Third World Approach to Democracy*. Manila: Ministry of Public Information, 1982.

_____. *The Third Alternative*. Manila: Ministry of Public Information, 1980.

Mijares, Primitivo. *The Conjugal Dictatorship of Ferdinand and Imelda Marcos I*. San Francisco: Union Square Publications, 1976.

National Democratic Front. *Program of the National Democratic Front*. Revised draft Manila, 1985.

Niksch, Larry A., and Niehaus, Marjorie. *The Internal Situation in the Philippines: Current Trends and Future Prospects*. Washington D.C.: Congressional Research Service, The Library of Congress, January 20, 1981.

Philippine Resource Center. *Sourcebook on the Philippine Economic Crisis: Analysis and Clippings*. Berkeley: Philippine Resource Center, 1984.

Poole, Fred, and Vanzi, Max. *Revolution in the Philippines: The United States in a Hall of Cracked Mirrors*. New York: McGraw-Hill Book Company, 1984.

Psinakis, Steve. *Two "Terrorists" Meet*. San Francisco: Alchemy Books, 1981.

Rosenberg, David A., ed. *Marcos and Martial Law in the Philippines*. Ithaca, New York: Cornell University Press, 1979.

Salonga, Jovito R. "The Marcos Dictatorship and a Vision of Government." Unpublished ms. [Los Angeles, 1984].

Salonga, Jovito R.; De la Costa, Horacio, et al. *A Message of Hope to Filipinos Who Care: Containing an Analysis of Three Years of Martial Law.* Manila, October 1, 1975.

Spence, Hartzell. *Marcos of the Philippines.* New York: World Publishing Co., 1969.

Steinberg, David Joel. *The Philippines: A Singular and a Plural Place.* Boulder, Colorado: Westview Press, 1982.

Thompson, W. Scott. *Unequal Partners: Philippine and Thai Relations with the United States, 1965-1975.* Lexington, Mass.: D.C. Heath, 1975.

U.S. Congress. Senate. Committee on Foreign Relations. *The Situation in the Philippines: A Staff Report Prepared by Frederick Z. Brown and Carl Ford for the Committee on Foreign Relations.* [98th Cong., 2nd sess.], 1984.

The following sources (journals and periodicals) are useful:

Asian Studies
Asian Survey
Far Eastern Economic Review
Foreign Affairs
Foreign Policy
Los Angeles Times
New York Times
Pacific Affairs
Philippine News
San Francisco Chronicle
San Francisco Examiner
Southeast Asian Affairs (annual)

Index

About the Author

ALBERT F. CELOZA is on the Faculty of Social Sciences at Phoenix College and an adjunct professor in International Studies at the American Graduate School of International Management Thunderbird and an affiliate with the Program for Southeast Asian Studies, Arizona State University. He holds degrees from the University of the Philippines, the University of San Francisco and the Claremont Graduate School.

ISBN 0-275-94137-X